## About the Author

Penelope lives in a pretty village in Kent, the English county known as 'The Garden of England'. She has two grown up sons and a little dog called Dora.

Trained as a Registered Nurse and tutor, she travelled the world for three years as a Nursing Officer, before retiring in order to paint and to write.

# Nurse on Board
## Part One
## Northern Seas

# Penelope Skilbeck

# Nurse on Board
## Part One
## Northern Seas

Olympia Publishers
*London*

# www.olympiapublishers.com
## OLYMPIA PAPERBACK EDITION

A CIP catalogue record for this title is
available from the British Library.

ISBN: 978-1-78830-697-3

First Published in 2021

Olympia Publishers
Tallis House
2 Tallis Street
London
EC4Y 0AB
Printed in Great Britain

# Dedication

For
Oliver and Rupert

# Part 1

# Chapter 1

## *In the beginning*

I had been training Nursing Assistants and other Ancillary workers at the Kent and Canterbury Hospital. I am a restless being, probably as a result of being a child of the Colonies, our family had never been able to stay anywhere long; and 5 years was my usual limit in a job before boredom set in. I was 57 and beginning to wonder what to do next, when one of my students announced that she had landed a job on a Cruise Liner! Now I have always loved the sea, possibly because the family had sailed to Port Said in Egypt, on the Strathnaver before I was a year old, so my earliest impressions must have come from ships; the constant throb of the engines, the whole ship endlessly groaning and creaking, as it endeavoured to stay in one piece despite the forces of wind and wave, and the long shiny cream painted corridors. I do remember as a six-year-old, sailing to Singapore on the Troop Ship 'Empire Windrush', the ship famous for bringing over the much-needed Caribbean immigrant workers after the war. When we were on her, she had engine failure and we were becalmed in the Red Sea, it was so hot, the troops turned hoses onto us children. Great fun. I have a picture of my brother and myself, me, in a nylon bubble swimming costume, my brother in woollen trunks. The Windrush sank soon after in March 1954 when there was an engine explosion, and she caught fire, so they had to abandon ship 'women and children first', then the gentlemen, some wearing bowler hats and doing comedy jumps into the sea. Four crew died in the explosion, but everybody else got off. I remember my parents talking about it, particularly the danger of the Nurse Sharks, which were supposed to be very ferocious in that region.

That didn't put me off and there was little else to stop me! My children had flown and were both doing post-graduate courses, my dogs had departed to doggy heaven and I just had 'The Cat.' I set to methodically and managed to get a job as a Nursing Officer within a few weeks! It was important to me that the ships were 'proper', ships that looked like ships and not blocks of flats. They seemed happy with my advanced years, valuing the experience it gave me, which was refreshing. Indeed, I was well qualified for this particular job, mainly because my very restlessness had given me a wide experience of the different areas of Nursing, but also because I understood the services and the 'Ranking' system.

I just had to settle 'The Cat.' Sadly, my brother-in-law and his wife had just lost theirs to old age and were persuaded to take William. He was a rescue and I felt particularly guilty at passing him on when I had promised he had a home for life, I have never given an animal away before and cried all the way home after leaving him with them. He must have felt so betrayed. But I knew he had a good home. Indeed, he became very fat and contented, living to a ripe old age.

My new company had three Cruise ships when I joined,

and added another just as I finished. A small one which had been a car ferry was only about 11,000 tonnes taking around four hundred passengers. It was particularly popular with an older group of British who had sailed on her repeatedly. It had a basic water sports area on the original drive-on platform at the stern. However, because most of the passengers were aged, on the rare occasion it was used, the crew had a whale of a time, being towed on the Banana Boat and using the Jet Ski's. The middle-sized Ship, around twenty-four thousand tonnes and holding around eight hundred passengers, and, my favourite, twenty-six thousand tonnes and eight hundred passengers. Towards the end of my time a new one of twenty-eight thousand tonnes was added. Since then, the small one has been scrapped and replaced with an even larger one of forty-three thousand tons. However, they are all pretty ships that have proper prows that cut through the waves with panache, together with smart bridges!

The Norwegian company has a particular attachment to all things British, emanating from the days of Nazi Occupation when in 1940 two hundred refugees were welcomed to Shetland. From then on, a clandestine Special Operations group made a permanent link between Norway and Shetland using fishing boats and disguised submarines, it became known as 'The Shetland Bus.'

At my interview I was told I would have to undergo a 'little' Seaman's training. This would entail a few days at a specialist facility at Walsash near Southampton and I drove down greatly excited. I was given passable 'Officer' accommodation and I met my fellow trainees in the 'Mess' They were a mixture of recruits, Shop Assistants, Hairdressers and other Ship specialisms. One girl who was obviously on a refreshment course, heard which company I was with and said, that she was always amused to look down on our 'little' ships from her lofty ones. The first day was about 'abandoning ship' and was conducted in the pool where we had to climb into a life raft from the water. Very difficult for an elderly lady with a slightly dickey knee! Then we had to leave the life-raft, form a circle holding hands in the water facing out-wards, in order to kick at any passing sharks! and finally we had to jump off a five metre board in a simulated storm, noise, wind and rain, all very realistic, wearing a life jacket which you had to hold tightly against your chest, in order not to break your neck on impact with the water!

The next day started well enough with a morning lecture on fire hazards and theory, something I had been through many times in different hospitals, however in the afternoon, we had a practical fire exercise. This entailed suiting up in full fireproof gear and wearing breathing apparatus. I am 5'2" at my tallest, and quite well endowed, the suit was a little tight!

We were to climb into a smoke-filled burning 'ship' and search in the correct fashion, holding hands and sweeping blindly for a 'body'. I was breathing too fast and running out of air, mainly because it was so hot, my suit was tight and my boobs were scorching!

After we had rescued the 'body' we had to cool a shaft using hoses, climb down said shaft and put out a fire in a room below. The trouble was I had oxygen cylinders on my back and hot boobs at the front, I got stuck! I had to be pushed from above until I popped through the hatch like a cork! I kept pointing out to anybody who would listen, that if there was a fire on board I would be at the end of the line receiving the injured, not fighting the b… fire!

# Chapter 2

## *On Board*

My new job started almost the moment I boarded an airplane from Manchester to the Caribbean. I was standing in the rear of the plane trying to find my seat when I overheard a gentleman on the phone to the company's offices in Ipswich. I could tell that he was being told that the new nurse was on board! My first patient awaited me!

There wasn't much I could do for a lady who had clearly had some sort of ischaemic attack. I had no equipment on me, so the airport Nurse was called and the patient was found to have a very high blood pressure, so she and her companion were disembarked. So disappointing for them, but it was a long flight.

After the initial drama, the flight was uncomplicated and gave me the opportunity to make myself known to a couple of the company representatives who were accompanying the passengers on the scheduled flight. After eight hours we arrived at Bridgetown, Barbados.

## Bridgetown, Barbados

It was wonderfully warm after a dreary English winter. We boarded buses to transfer to the ship, which allowed us to see a little of the island; wonderful tropical foliage, little brightly painted wooden houses with 'stoops' to the front and of course the turquoise sea and high blue sky. We arrived at the ship and embarked in orderly fashion.

Our elegant ship was dwarfed by a nearby giant cruise liner, nonetheless she carried around a thousand crew and passengers. On board she appeared remarkably spacious with a beautiful glittering tall atrium, enormous murals and a grand staircase. There was a main lounge with a stage and bar; a grand dining room, several restaurants and small lounges, and more bars. There was a swimming pool, shops and hairdressers. I was very impressed.

My own quarters were not quite so spacious, appearing more like a Hobbit Hole. Probably no more than ten foot by six, with a narrow entrance containing the shower room and cupboard then through a curtain to the bunk and a desk. As a two-stripe officer, I was entitled to my own cabin with this tiny bathroom and the services of a stewardess. I could not have survived without this homely little retreat! Later I learned to make it my own with a rug and pictures.

The Medical Centre was in the middle of the ship and consisted of a consulting room, Office, and two small single wards. We carried a full Pharmacy and keeping this up to date and stocked was one of our duties. This Ship also had a Nurses Cabin actually in the centre which was currently occupied by a delightful Philippino nurse, Pearly and her Steward husband. How they squeezed in I don't know. I subsequently had that cabin on other trips, it was windowless, small and hot. There was a bell on the outside door and of course the occupant, always available!

We ran Doctor surgeries for passengers and crew twice daily and the nurses were on call for 24 hours each in turn. We could always bleep the Doctor if needed. Other duties were testing the water and ice every day for any sign of contamination and the shower-heads regularly for the dreaded 'Legionnaire's disease'.

My first evening on board was a whirl of meeting people with impossible Norwegian and Philippino names, finding my way around the nine decks, learning the emergency codes — Code Alpha, medical emergency and one I would get well used to! Code Bravo, fire, and Code Sierra, oil spill. These were called over the ships tannoy and were supposed to be only understood by the crew, in order not to worry the passengers. However, they quickly cottoned on as every time an Alpha was called the medical officers, having a quiet (soft) drink at the bar, looking like startled hamsters, would scuttle off with bleeps going. If somebody fell overboard, you had to point and keeping your eyes and finger fixed on them, shout 'Man Overboard'; fortunately, that one never happened during my sojourn. I was introduced to Kathy, the nurse I was joining who was to be a tower of strength. She had obviously been lacking company and talked non-stop. I was to rely on her enormously in the first few weeks. I also met our new doctor, an attractive man from the Scottish Borders, he had his pretty, slim, blond wife and ten-year-old son with him. In those days, the Doctor was usually a GP, booked just for the cruise. He made a little from the charges and had a free holiday for himself and the family. I had been up 25 hours by now and was keen to find my little cabin.

Next day I had to get my evening uniforms sorted out. We wore normal Nursing dresses during the day, navy for the north and white for warmer climes! We had the 'informal' one for most evenings, consisting of a short navy skirt and jacket which had two gold stripes on the sleeves, with a white shirt and a sort of bow tie pinned with a pearl stud. Then there was one for 'formal' evenings. This was a long black skirt with a short waisted white jacket with gold braided epaulets and the same bow tie. Now as mentioned before, I am short, narrow shouldered and well endowed, many of the female officers were little Philippino ladies. It was impossible! I had to have a man's jacket with broad shoulders. I looked a fright! On my next leave I pinched one and had it altered by a tailor at home. Still it is not my usual style!

My first trip was crossing the Atlantic back to the UK, this took six days to the Canaries and another three home. The first two days at sea were pleasant enough. We had a 'Code Alpha' when a woman fainted and another when a woman got drunk and fell off a bar stool at 2.00 a.m. No lasting damage for either. When a 'Code Alpha' was called the whole medical team of three rushed to the scene together with extra crew members who carried equipment, defibrillators and such. So, everybody got disturbed! In the early days my main problem was finding my way to the emergency. I still had to think which way was port, or starboard!

However, the remainder of the passengers gave us few anxious moments. Mainly it was seasickness, I got very skilled at crawling around tiny bathrooms, with a patient draped over the loo, trying to find an appropriate bit of buttock in which to inject the magical anti-emetic! We also had to deal with the dreaded D & V bug, Noro-virus, which haunts all cruise ships. This was quickly quashed by the extraordinary measures taken by the household members of the crew, with handrails being wiped half hourly and spoons changed continually in the restaurants. We had strict barrier nursing and sufferers were confined to their cabins for several days. The virus itself is short lived so the continued confinement was a constant problem, once the passenger was feeling well it was difficult to insist that they had to stay in the cabin for two more days; the virus can be shed from a recovered patient for up to 72 hours, so it was necessary. However, being new, I was one of them, I succumbed to this horrid virus and spent two days in my bunk. It did give me a resistance and although I managed many of these outbreaks I only succumbed once more in three years.

I had been pleasantly surprised to find I didn't have a problem with seasickness. I had once been horribly sick on a yacht in Portugal. However, if it was rough, I kept taking the tablets and they seemed to work; as time went on, I needed them less, but rough seas would continue to be labelled by us nurses as a one or two Stugeron storm! The first time I went ashore, in the Canaries, after six days at sea I was really 'land sick' and very unstable. This only happened the once. Very strange.

We had a final three days at sea, braving the Bay of Biscay, which can be choppy. However, on this occasion it was behaving itself; and so, to Southampton. Offload the passengers and Dry Dock.

# Chapter 3

## *Dry Dock Southampton*

What can I say about Dry Dock? It is a refurbishment and general repair of all the ship including its bottom, sorry hull. It was quite interesting, getting into the dock! It really didn't look as if we would fit, but inch by inch, we crept in and were tied up. The water was drained and the poor ship was left high and dry. Very undignified for her. We were marooned for a week, with hundreds of workmen crawling all over the ship, endless plastic covering in all the passenger areas, no air conditioning, lavatories only working intermittently and miles of blue piping containing unmentionable things! Pearly, my Philippino colleague, and I ran a daily clinic for the crew, who all had colds, just because we were in Southampton! My elder son came to visit, but the Docks are so endless and featureless that he couldn't find me. I wasn't able to describe to him where we were. I had only been 'ashore' once, teetering across a plank and taking a Taxi into town. However, we eventually met up and had a nice meal of Lobster Thermador in the Officers Mess (I think they were trying to compensate for the uncomfortable conditions we were living in!). Pearly and I spent the rest of the time stocktaking every pill and potion in the place, and sleeping!

However, we still had to have our weekly drill. Slightly different because we were to practice evacuating the ship to the dockside instead of into the boats. I was in trouble as the only one who didn't take my life jacket! After all there's no water in 'Dry dock'!

Dry Dock finished. The ship came to life with a miraculous speed. The dock was refilled and she shot out like a cork from a bottle. Ready for the next Cruise.

# Chapter 4

## *Mini Cruises*

### Guernsey

Situated in the English Channel, just off the coast of Normandy, Guernsey remains a Crown Dependency. Occupied by Neolithic Farmers, as far back as BC 5000, they left Dolman's or Tombs, piles of enormous stones, scattered around the countryside. Roman 'Amphorae' from Herculaneum have been discovered, suggesting an intricate trading network. Archaeologists have also found signs of what are thought to have been early warehouses from this period. During the middle ages the islands belonged to France, becoming a haven for Pirates who used 'Lamping' to lure ships onto the rocks, so they could be pillaged. The enormous 'Castle Cornet' was started in 1206, built on a little promontory island. After the 'Hundred Years War' with France, 1339–1439, Pope Sixtus IV granted the 'Privilege of Neutrality' to the Islands. A Royal Charter confirmed this in 1548. The French didn't like this very much and made several attempts to invade, but they were fought off by the 'Royal

Guernsey Militia' who were loyal to the British Crown. This 'charter' held until the 17th century when King William III, also known as 'William of Orange', revoked it because of the Privateering against Dutch Ships.

Threats from Napoleon prompted more fortifications, including several 'Martello Towers'. There are also 15 slightly prettier 'Loophole Towers', built in 1778–79 with tiny windows, which were probably gun placements.

During WWII Guernsey was occupied, together with Jersey, by the Germans and there are massive fortifications from this period all over the islands. One thousand residents were deported to a camp in southern Germany. The Islands were liberated in 1945 it was the only part of the British Isles to fall to Germany.

We had to tender to St Peter Port, which means lowering the lifeboats and using them to transport passengers ashore. I needed to escort a gentleman who had had a heart attack to the local hospital. Very modern and bright. Thank goodness it was calm, there had been occasions here, when it was too rough to tender the passengers ashore.

Such an attractive town with very steep streets; crowded with visitors, though there was little traffic. I was told that there are fewer than 5,000 people on Guernsey, no more than a large village. There were some fabulous shoes and clothes in the shops, very expensive. The island is only nine miles long and three wide. The weather was warm with hundreds of little boats in the harbour. I particularly liked the blue post boxes.

Victor Hugo was exiled here in 1885 and wrote some of his best-known books, including 'Les Misérables'. Renoir also came in 1833, painting many pictures of the beaches.

They have the famous gentle Guernsey Cow and the

beautiful but less known 'Golden Guernsey Goat'. Saved from extinction by a woman called Miriam Melbourne, who hid her herd from the Germans during the war, in order to prevent inbreeding.

We could see Jersey, Herme and Sark from the Ship.

## Antwerp, Belgium

There may have been a Roman settlement here. Archaeologists have turned up a variety of artefacts including roman glass. There is some controversy as to how it got its name, but the story I like is that of a giant called Antigone, who lived by extracting tolls from passing boatmen. If they refused, he cut of one of their hands throwing it in the river. A young Roman hero named Salvius Brabo managed to put a stop to that. Somehow, he contrived to cut off the giant's hand and threw it into the river. Antwerpen is 'hand' in Dutch. There is a statue to them both in front of the City Hall. The 16th century, was called the 'Golden Age', the city becoming the busiest and most prosperous in northern Europe. Banking and manufacturing thrived. However, things started to go wrong around 1668, when during the 80 years' war, in which the Dutch and Spanish were having a go at each other, the place was sacked. This incident became known as 'The Spanish Fury'. Apparently, Philip II of Spain, ran out of money and couldn't pay his troops, partly because our Queen Elizabeth I had seized 400,000 florins, when the Spanish ships carrying them were sheltering from a storm in English harbours. This money was their pay and so the Spanish Army got cross and, taking things into their own hands, decided to loot what they could. Antwerp lost 7,000 civilians and 800 houses were burnt down.

It was quite a long cruise up the River Schelat which is heavily industrialized, busy with shipping of all sorts, a bit like dodgems! Our mooring was right is the centre of the city. There was a hold-up with the docking as the Belgians wanted us to use their tugs. Our captain didn't consider them necessary; he was very proud of his bow thrusters! Small international incident!

We remained docked overnight and a lot of passengers and crew went ashore for their evening meal. I was on duty, so had to wait until the next day. I heard reports from some of the younger English crew that they were not welcomed in the clubs! A remnant of football hooliganism or the Iraqi war, we couldn't decide which. If you said you were Scottish or Irish, that was OK!

Next morning after clinic I made straight for the 14th century Cathedral of 'Our Lady', an enormous edifice in the centre of the old city. It has a very tall and elegant spire. Vast inside, with a wonderful Rubens Triptych behind the Alter. There is also an ornately carved Pulpit covered in animals, birds and foliage. At Noon the bells play a veritable concert; very pretty. The main square, Grote Makt, has the impressive 16th century City Hall taking up one side with a row of International flags in front. The other three sides are filled with ancient tall skinny Flemish Guild houses sporting ornately stepped gables and fancy brickwork. Most are only about one room wide, but about eight stories' high. There is also the oldest Stock Exchange in the world. Built in 1531 and rebuilt, after a fire in 1872. It's tucked away behind Twaalfmaandenstraat. In a bit of a state now, but under renovation.

The cobbles are large, uneven and full of potholes; there are masses of Chocolate and beer shops. I enjoyed the former, but also spent some time watching a bobbin lace-making demonstration. Extremely fine and very expensive. I bought a little mat, to start a collection of lace from around the world. I would have loved to visit the famous diamond district. Antwerp is one of the most important diamond cutting centres in the world. I didn't risk it.

Later, some friends and I visited the beer cellars, many of these are medieval. Low coved ceilings and lots of candle smoke. I had a cherry beer, quite pleasant. Outside we saw a wonderful pair of Flemish Giant Horses pulling an old horse bus for the tourists.

Many famous people have either been born or have lived here, particularly artists, who came to study at the art schools. The pre-Raphaelite painter Ford Maddox Brown and Robert Browning are just two.

## Back to Dover for a turnaround

Very hard work for the crew, but especially the Housekeeping. Passengers offloaded in the morning and new ones welcomed warmly in the afternoon. This left a very short time to clean and prepare the 600 to 1,000 cabins, depending on the ship. The whole ship has to be re-provisioned, including water, food and all things domestic. The shops have to restock and so did we in the medical centre. There was often a change of crew as well, and a bus load of mostly Philippinos would arrive and another go home to their families for a month or so. They had quite long contracts of about nine months on board; leaving their children in the care of grandmothers. It seemed sad, but was a tradition in the Philippines, a seafaring nation.

I had a good 'gang' of friends coming on board. Paula, a new Hotel Manager, Sue a great Cruise Director and my old friend Sally who used to be Shop Manager, but who was now making a spectacular success of being tours Manager. The Hotel Manager is in charge of all the housekeeping side of things and the Cruise Director is in charge of entertainment, they are both senior officers. We called ourselves the 'WI' and had some fun evenings.

I celebrated my sixtieth birthday on board. Kindnesses from my colleagues ranged from a Helicopter trip in Funchal to an evening in the Officers Mess with balloons, 'prezzies', Champagne and an alcoholic chocolate cake with a chocolate syringe on top! Made by the Chef. The Captain was there and everybody went to a lot of trouble.

# Chapter 5

## *Around the British Isles*

### Falmouth, Cornwall

We had just battled our way through the Bay of Biscay in a force nine, with storm gusts to ten. It has been a dreadful night but surprisingly no calls! This was towards the end of a cruise which had been relentlessly rough, I think the passengers were resigned and just desperate to get home in one-piece. I had a loose oxygen cylinder rattling around in a cupboard next to my cabin but couldn't face battling with it. Just hanging on to one's bunk made it impossible to sleep anyway. My spectacles, which were on a table next to my bunk slipped, unnoticed by me, and wedged themselves between my mattress and the bunk surround, breaking badly. It must have been an unusual insurance claim. Glasses broken in a storm at sea.

Falmouth is an attractive town, a few steep roads down to the harbour; the third deepest in the world and one which has seen many famous ships including the Beagle when it returned from its surveying trip to Australasia with Darwin on board. The town was built by Sir John Killigrew in 1613 which would explain a certain cohesion in the architecture, more rugged than I was expecting. I think I was anticipating a reflection of the softer climate of Cornwall. Henry VIII built the Circular Pendennis Castle at the mouth of what is called Carrick Roads, a disingenuous name for what is an estuary leading to the River Fal. The castle was built to protect against the threat of French invasion and later the Spanish and the Holy Roman Empire, who were all pretty cross with Henry.

During the Civil war, Pendennis was one of the last castles to surrender to the Parliamentarians. After the Restoration in 1660 Sir Peter Killigrew gave land for a Church to be built naming it 'King Charles the Martyr'. There is a strange pyramid style monument to Sir Peter in Arwenack street.

The Packet Service, taking mail to the empire, was run from here for 160 years. Some of the town's history is displayed in the National Maritime Museum in the harbour. There is also the lovely Kimberley Park, full of the exotic trees and plants they are able to grow in the mild climate of Cornwall. The Falmouth Art Gallery is also worth a visit.

## Waterford, Ireland

The name Waterford is derived from an old Norse word meaning Ram. It is the oldest city in the Republic of Ireland and was originally established by Viking Raiders in 853 AD. However, they were driven out in 902 AD by the locals who soon managed to re-established themselves and hung on until in 1171 AD Richard de Clare, together with some Welsh-Norman mercenaries and King Henry II finally drove them out and declared the place a Royal City. It was a major port for a thousand years with Shipbuilding being the primary industry. Today it is known for Waterford Crystal, a legacy of an earlier glass making industry. I could see the old Reginald Tower from the ship, which retains its original Viking name but not its original defensive purpose, today it is a Civic Museum, part of the Waterford Museum of Treasures.

Unfortunately, we had one of our weekly crew drills. I was assigned a lifeboat rather than a life-raft, thank goodness. If we had to 'Abandon Ship', my job would be to look after the medical needs of those in my boat. This would be difficult, with passengers packed tightly on the seats under which the medical supplies were stashed. I would have to get at these immediately because the sea would most likely be very rough and I would need to get the seasickness tablets out. It could never be quick enough; everyone would be vomiting pretty much as soon as we hit the water!

Despite the drill I managed a short time ashore, and what I did see of Waterford surprised me. The houses are all painted in bright colours, no holds barred. I saw orange, lavender, bright blues and reds. Somehow, I had expected it to be dour and Celtic. There appears to be a pattern emerging here of my expectations never meeting the realities on this trip. The Christ Church Cathedral, built on the site of two much earlier ones in the 18th century, has a certain gravitas, together with the Bishops Palace and the Medieval Museum, all these together with Reginald's Tower, are part of what is known as the Viking Triangle.

## Cobh, Ireland

The name Cobh is a gallicisation of the word Cove and is actually pronounced 'cove'. It was renamed 'Queenstown' between 1849 and 1920 to commemorate Queen Victoria visiting Ireland, but once the old girl died it reverted to its original name. Cobh lies on the south side of what is called 'Great Island'. Legend says the first colonizer of Ireland, a chap called Neimhedh, landed in the harbour at Cobh in around BC 1000. Unfortunately, these early settlers all died of Plague.

Cobh became an important military base right from the Napoleonic and through to the French Wars of 1778–1783. Much of the town's elegant architecture dates from this period, including the old Cove Fort to the east of the town, which dates from 1743. There are two pretty islands sitting in the harbour, Spike Island and Haulbowline. Haulbowline is the site of the earliest Yacht club in the world. Originally called 'The Water Club' it was first set up in 1720. Eask Tower built in 1847, as a guide for shipping, sits on Carhoo hill overlooking the harbour, a short hike for the energetic.

There is a history of shipbuilding, but also one of tragedy. The Titanic departed from Cobh for her ill-fated Maiden voyage in 1912, there is a memorial to this in Westbourne Place. The town later had to bury a hundred bodies from the Lusitania which was torpedoed on its way from the U.S.A during WWII. It was the departure point for Felons and criminals who were deported to the Penal Colonies and also for the millions of the population escaping the potato famine, emigrating around the world. There is a touching statue at the dock gates of somebody called Anne Moore and her two brothers. They were the first people to be admitted to America via Ellis Island.

The Cathedral Spire of St Colman's dominates the town, built in 1867, it has a carillon of 49 bells and is one of the tallest buildings in Ireland.

I went to a 'Traditional Irish Night' put on for us tourists, in a lovely converted Jameson distillery. There was a table set up for tasting the various whiskey's, hundreds of tiny glasses set in rows, they were surprisingly different in taste and colour, but I'm not a neat whiskey drinker. The passengers enjoyed it and sang all the way back to the ship. I was introduced to Murphy's beer, which I did rather like!

Other places of interest include the new 'Titanic Experience.' The Cobh Heritage Centre, near the railway station and tours to Haulbowline. A little to the northwest of the town on the headland called Gallarus is an ancient dry-stone Oratory of the same name, it has sloping sides and is thought to be around 1,000 years old, enchanting and rather otherworldly, with seagulls screaming in the wind.

## Dingle, County Kerry, Ireland

Sitting out on its own little peninsular on the Atlantic coast between Tralee and Killarney, the little port town was settled following the Norman Invasion of Ireland, rapidly developing into an important port with strong connections to Spain. Pilgrims would embark from here for the Camino de Santiago pilgrimage to Northern Spain. From the 14th century they had monopolized the import of wine and by the 16th century the town had become Ireland's main trading port, exporting fish and hides as well as importing those wines.

From 1597 to 1583, there were two major rebellions, known as the Desmond Rebellions in which the FitzGerald dynasty of local big-wigs fought against the English intrusion of their territories, trying to retain both Catholicism and their

Irish culture, whilst endeavouring to wrest control from the English Queen Elizabeth I, mightily upsetting her. The town was granted the right to build a Wall, some of which can still be seen today. The result was the crushing of the Desmond dynasty and the introduction of more English 'Planters', or settlers.

After all the sacking and burning of this little town, in 1820 a local philanthropist, one of the Fitzgerald's, imported some Flax seed and shared it out. Re-establishing an ancient industry, a thriving Linen business grew until the Industrialization of the cotton mills in England caused its demise.

Now a bright and colourful little holiday town on a peninsular with lovely beaches and a small busy harbour which has a resident Dolphin, Fungie. The main street shops and houses are painted in yellows, blues and purples. I found a wonderful old Linen shop, all that is left of a once flourishing industry, I bought a small bobbin lace mat to add to my collection of laces from around the world.

## Cleggan

A picturesque fishing village in County Galway, it sits in a little bay and has a small pier, built in 1822 and extended in 1908 from which the ferries depart daily for the nearby islands of Inishark, Shark island, and Inishbofin, meaning Island of the white Cow. There was a monastery dating from around 665 AD on the latter, set up by St Colman, then later, a fort where Cromwell imprisoned Catholics.

Cleggan meaning 'head' or 'skull' presumably because of the shape of its headland. However, there is a much more gruesome and therefore more interesting story in which a local Saint called Ceannanach beheaded a local pagan Chieftain and after washing the said head in a holy well, for some reason decided to lay down to die. At the top of Cleggan head there are some remains, but only of a Napoleonic Watch tower. The existence of prehistoric Standing stones, walls and tombs nearby, indicate the area has been inhabited 'forever'.

We are by now half way up the west coast, a wild coastline with lots of little islands. Not as rugged as the Scottish isles, but just as treeless. The hinterland has areas of 'Blanket Bog', a unique type of peat bog, the last of its type to survive in Europe.

In 1927 there was a major Disaster called the 'Cleggan Bay disaster' in which a storm blew up and drowned nearly all the local fishermen who were busy Mackerel fishing at the time. The nearby village of Rossadilisk lost sixteen of its twenty-five breadwinners and was abandoned. The area was devastated and became one of the earliest national appeals, with which we are now so familiar. The disaster is immortalized in literature and song to this day.

We have had to Tender at these last two ports and it has not been easy getting our rather frail and elderly passengers on and off the tenders during a large swell. One has to leap at just the appropriate moment, between the ship and the tender so the poor seamen have to hang on to the passengers and push them at the 'appropriate moment', hoping the crew on the Tender catch them at the 'appropriate moment', and we all hope we see the 'appropriate moment' at the same time! We haven't lost anyone yet.

# Killybegs

The name Killybegs is Gaelic for 'little cells', referring to the small stone huts or cells, that were used by early Monks, remains of which have been found in the area. Situated in County Donegal, the scenic deep-water harbour is the second largest fishing port in Ireland, it can take the largest of the pelagic trawlers and has a significant fishing and fish processing industry. It's situated at the base of a mountain range which extends right up to the north. In 1588 some of the Spanish Armada sheltered here, including the ship La Girona, which was repaired with the help of a local chieftain. However, on its way up to Scotland, it foundered with great loss of life and treasure. The treasure was finally recovered by a Belgium team in 1967–68, the finest ever recovered from an Armada Ship. The gold jewellery is now in the Ulster Museum in Belfast.

The town has a street festival in the summer, celebrating the fish catches and 'blessing' the boats. There was also an important industry in high quality 'knotted' carpets and tapestries, one of the factories had the largest loom in the world and their carpets adorn many of the most important buildings in the world, including Buckingham Palace. Unfortunately, it closed down in 2003, opening again in 2006 as a Maritime and Heritage centre.

The town is neat, with wide streets and a certain coherence in its architecture. The Church spire of St Mary of the Visitation, is tall and slim, floating over the simple houses. Nearby is St Catherine's Well together with the remains of the 12th century Church. The St Catherine in this case is the Martyr, St Catherine of Alexandria. Kitts Castle on the little hill next to these is really the remains of a 14th century Manor House used by the Bishops.

We went south east to the town of Donegal, the name means 'Port of the Foreigner'; it's situated on the mouth of the River Eske. Archaeological evidence in the form of defensive earthworks, suggests that there have been settlements here from prehistory. There's the impressive Donegal Castle with its square Keep dating back to the 15th century with later Jacobean additions. It was the seat of the all-powerful O'Donnell dynasty, one the richest and most influential families in Donegal from the 13th to the beginning of the 17th century when the 'Nine Years War', an Irish rebellion against the English, erupted. Unfortunately, the Irish lost and the Castle was seized for the English Crown and given to an English 'Planter' named Capt. Basil Brook. He extended the Castle and laid out the town as we see it now, including the attractive Diamond Square, with the 'Four Masters Memorial Obelisk' which honours four scribes from the nearby Franciscan Friary, now in ruins.

It was one of the worst hit areas during the potato famine of 1845–49 and much of the area was permanently depopulated. There is a famine graveyard in Ballybofey Road on the edge of town. Partition was another blow as it separated Donegal from Derry which had been its main trading partner for centuries. Despite all this it remains a handsome town.

We were on our way to the famous Belleek factory. As a collector of this fine white china, I was eager to see where it was made. Apparently, it was started in the mid-19th century, by a gentleman called John Caldwell Bloomfield, a philanthropist, who was looking to provide employment following the devastation of the potato famine. He was an amateur mineralogist and noticed the fine white clay in the area, together with the unusual minerals that go towards producing the glistening pearlized glazes that make the china so special. Although I collect older pieces, some of which I found in New Zealand, presumably taken there by immigrants, I allowed myself to buy a large Cornucopia vase.

There are two attractive churches, St Patricks Church, a very pretty 1930's confection with a thin round tower amongst steep angled roofs and the simple Gothic style 'Church of Ireland,' built in the 1820's. The bay itself is home to a colony of Seals and has both Cormorants and Cranes.

## Bangor and the Giants Causeway

Bangor is a large seaside and commuter town for Belfast, its name probably means 'curved horn' reflecting the shape of the bay. Situated in County Down, and south of the sizable Belfast Lough. Archaeological artefacts have been found from the bronze age. St Comgall founded a rather austere Monastery here in around 558 AD. This Monastery was very influential in establishing the church in Ireland and one of the first places to train Missionaries. Bangor, originally called Inver Beg, is one of only four places to be named in the Hereford Mappa Mundi.

Not much of the Monastery remains today, just a piece of wall called St Malachy's Wall, the church on the site does have a tower dating back to the 14th century and the Monastery's Sundial now sits outside the Town Hall. Sometimes called The Vale of the Angels, it's said that St Patrick rested here and saw Angels in the Valley. Later, during the 8th and 9th centuries, like much of Ireland, they suffered from violent Viking raids.

Modern Bangor town has its origins in the early 17th century, when James Hamilton, a lowland Scot, was granted lands here by James VI of Scotland and I of England in 1605. He developed the town and built the Old Custom House of Bangor, on the seafront, with its round tower adjoining Tower House. The place prospered throughout the 18th century, largely due to its cotton milling industry, but as that floundered, it became fashionable to take the 'sea air' and the Victorians started holidaying here. The elegant seafront is largely Victorian and at the bottom of the high-street is the Marina, one of the largest in Ireland. In the Marina's Sunken gardens is the handsome McKee Clock, named after a local benefactor.

During WWII President Eisenhower addressed the Allied troops here, prior to them leaving for the D day landings. The North Pier has been re-named Eisenhower Pier.

On the North coast of County Antrim, we visited the Giants Causeway, this extraordinary geological site with its pillars of hexagonal Basalt rocks is supposed to be the result of volcanic activity millions of years ago. I prefer the story of Fin Macool, an Irish Giant, who built the causeway so that a Scottish Giant and he could 'do battle'. However, when Fin saw the size of his opponent, he became afraid so his wife hid him by putting him in a cradle, pretending he was a baby. When the Scottish Giant saw the size of the 'baby' he was afraid to meet the father of such an infant and ran back to Scotland, breaking up the causeway as he went!

Going as an 'Escort' on passenger trips was an extra privilege, but also carried responsibilities, especially as I was always recognized as 'The Nurse'. On this trip I had to patch up a lady who fell getting down from the coach. Just a sticking plaster job fortunately.

We then went on to Bushmills Whiskey Distillery, the oldest 'legal' distillery in Ireland. I must say, probably sacrilegiously, that I didn't like it very much, preferring a Scottish blended whiskey. However, the process was interesting.

We had a good look at the countryside on the way back, the coastline around Antrim is most impressive, with dramatic cliffs and lovely wide sandy beaches.

## Dublin

Situated at the mouth of the River Liffey, the city is the Capital and the largest in Ireland. Considering itself to be a mere 1,000 years old, however there is archaeological evidence of an earlier Viking settlement and its thought that even the Vikings were probably preceded by an ecclesiastical establishment known as 'Duiblinn'. The Vikings, having got rid of the monks, ruled for the next 300 years until most of them were expelled in 1014 by the Irish King Brian, although he was chased and killed soon after the battle. After which the Vikings became an insignificant minority. Those who did remain built their own settlement on the north of the river, an area which became known as Oxmantown, where they continued to conduct a thriving slave trade, capturing and selling 'thralls' (serfs) right up until 1685. Dublin city became the Capital of the English 'Lordship of Ireland' from 1171. A compact city, the native Irish were forced outside the bounds into areas know as 'Liberties', a few of these medieval areas still exist.

There have been endless contenders for Dublin throughout its history, but the English took control when Henry VIII finally squashed the Fitzgerald clan the Earls of Kildare, who were in charge at the time, replacing them with English Administrators and encouraging more English 'Planters' to settle. Rebellions and unrest continued throughout the 16th century, compounded during the nine years war, when an English gunpowder store exploded, killing 200 Dubliners. During the Cromwellian conquest of Ireland, Catholics were banned from dwelling within the city.

There was rapid growth from the 17th century onward and during the 18th century, much of medieval Dublin was demolished, replaced by elegant Georgian thoroughfares and five city squares. It was during this period that moves toward union and Catholic emancipation began to develop. The Irish War of Independence of 1919–1921, during which the Irish Republican Army waged urban guerrilla warfare against the British Army, resulted in many tragic incidents on both sides.

Unfortunately, one had to travel through some rather ugly docklands to reach the city. My garrulous Taxi driver told me that there was a ten-year plan to improve the area, should be just about done by now. There was one rather lovely classical building on the north bank. Originally built during the 18th century as a customs house, it now holds a variety of government offices.

Despite the demolition of much of the centre during the early 20th century, to make room for modern commercial development, the city retains some lovely elegant Georgian buildings, including Trinity College with its impressive square, established in 1592, by Queen Elizabeth I and Dublin Castle, which still has its medieval tower and Chapel. Now known as Leinster House, the seat of the Oireachtas, or Parliament of Ireland.

It would have been nice to explore by myself, but I had

arranged to meet a group of friends for lunch, which we had in a very good 'Italian Restaurant'. We then went shopping in Grafton Street, lively and sophisticated with a statue of Molly Malone. There are various depictions of Molly, one that she was a Fish hawker by day and a prostitute by night and the other that she was a fish hawker by day and 'chaste' by night. Take your pick. St Stephens Green is a delightful park adjacent to Grafton street where there's a very modern 390ft tall stainless steel 'Spire of Dublin' which replaces the original Nelsons Column, blown up during some earlier troubles. Rather incongruously, next to it is the statue of Jim Larkin an Irish Republican and Trade Unionist. O'Connell Street is another important thoroughfare and Henrietta Street still has very grand red brick Georgian facades and is exceptionally wide.

I left my friends in a pub having a last Guinness as I had to take over on board to let another member of the medical team come ashore.

Just as well because later that evening, we had an emergency call to a lady who had fallen down a long flight of metal stairs leading into a crew area. We didn't know how she could possibly have done it; the staircase was roped off with a notice saying 'crew only'. When I first saw her, covered in blood and wedged at the bottom of the small stairwell I expected the worst. She was 85. The 'Code Alpha' crew managed to excavate her with great care and some difficulty, because we assumed that with such a fall, she must have broken something. However, on careful examination, we could only identify some nasty cuts to her head so the Doctor and I stitched her up, one on each side, she chatted right through it.

I then had the pleasure of nursing her overnight, although shocked, she didn't appear to be concussed, even so we did hospitalize her on docking in Liverpool the next morning.

## Kirkwall. Isle of Orkney

Situated on the north coast on Orkney the main island of the Scottish archipelago, Kirkwall is not named for the current Cathedral, but for an earlier, much smaller Church, named for St Olaf of Norway; very little is left of the original, which is in Dundas Crescent, just a door and an Aumbry, an aperture in the wall for storing things.

From around 1046 it was inhabited by Norse Jarls or Earls who named it Kirkuvjar or Church Bay. Its significance is noted in a medieval Norse Orkneyinga Saga which centres around Orkney. The Impressive Romanesque Magnus Cathedral, which dominates the little town, was started in 1108 and dedicated to St Magnus Erendsson another Earl of Orkney, built of a much redder stone than any of the other buildings, probably shipped from somewhere in France. Later it became the residence of Rognvald Brusason, who was killed by his uncle Thorfinn the Mighty in 1486. James III of Scotland having had enough of the squabbles elevated Kirkwall to the status of a Royal Burgh. Next to the Cathedral are the ruins of both the Bishops' and the Earls' palaces.

It has a very pretty protected harbour too small for our ship, so we tendered the passengers ashore. The Harbour front, has a row of substantial Scottish houses and an hotel, mainly 19th century, built of a solid dark granite. Behind these is Broad street, with its attractive rather smaller buildings. I went through a stone arch into the Orkney Museum situated opposite the Cathedral. It inhabits a wonderful 16th century house and had a presentation showing the ancient stone age dwellings on the island.

These are well worth a visit, there is the Tomb of Maeshowe, a Neolithic chambered cairn with a grave passage, thought to have been built around BC 2800, and the Ring of Brodgar, six miles north east of Stromness, a Neolithic Henge and impressive circle of thin standing stones. My favourite, Skara Brae, is on the west coast in the Bay of Skail. Eight clustered dwellings dated from BC 3180–2500. Sitting inside one of these it's possible to get an insight into an ancient lifestyle.

The rest of the town is quaint, and can only have a few thousand inhabitants. There are a couple of interesting Iron age grain stores or Souterrains, and 'The Grain Earth House' on the lower junction of Scott's Road. West of the town we find Rennibister Earth House.

Out in the countryside, there is not a tree in sight, the farmsteads, individual and isolated like so many pimples on the landscape. It must be so bleak in the winter! There was some evidence of what people do on the long winter nights, lots of local handicrafts for sale in the shops.

An important area for bird life, both seabirds and migrating birds, there are several reserves. There are seals on the beaches and if you are very lucky, you just might get to spot a Sea Otter.

Once again, I had to deliver a lady ashore, she had been suffering serious stomach cramps all night and the Doctor was afraid she might have an obstruction, so we had put a drip up and spent the night nursing her. I took her across in a tender, first thing, to the waiting ambulance. She was given an enema and returned to us later that day to finish her cruise. Pink faces all round.

Later that day, the weather deteriorated and it was touch and go getting the tenders in and all the elderly passengers back to the ship safely without them getting squished between the boat and the harbour wall.

## Lerwick Shetland Isles

Lerwick means Bay of Clay in old Norse and a descendant of this language known as Norn was spoken in the islands until the middle of the nineteenth century. I went on a scenic drive through Shetland to see the 3,000-year-old dwellings known as Clickimin Brock, a carefully restored, probably bronze age Brock set on a promontory in a Loch. It's a strangely beautiful landscape, totally lacking trees, except back in the town. Granite rises through the peat in gentle eruptions. There are some beautiful views from the coast of outlying islands and wonderful white sandy coves, sometimes with seals basking in the surf. The sea looked clear enough to be in the Caribbean, but the temperature was decidedly chilly with strong winds blowing, even though it was July. Lots of lovely Shetland Ponies and strangely coloured Shetland Sheep. Apparently, these swim across to the smaller islands for summer grazing.

## Stornoway, Isle of Lewis, Outer Hebrides

Founded by Vikings, Stornoway is the largest town in the Hebrides. The island was transferred to Sir James Matheson and his descendants by James VI and it was the Mathesons who built the large Neo Gothic Castle on the remains of a much older one. The castle is surrounded by woodland, unusual in what is otherwise a treeless landscape. It remained in this family until 1918 when it was sold to 1st Viscount Leverhulme, who having overstretched himself financially finally gifted the parish to the people.

A pretty town with an active fishing fleet, though the weather was rather bleak on our visit.

## Islay, Port Ellen

Islay is the southernmost island of the Inner Hebrides. Its Capital is Bowmore which has a distinctive round Parish Church at the top of its main street. It is yet another Island that has evidence of prehistoric occupation. It has changed hands many times, being part of the Gaelic Kingdom in the early middle ages, before being absorbed into the Norse 'Kingdom of the Isles' and then, in later medieval times being transferred to the Kingdom of Scotland and being handed over to the Clan Donald, Lordship of the Isles. Clan Donald faded in the seventeenth century and the Island moved through several Clans until in the nineteenth century the Campbells sold the Island to James Morrison of Berkshire, whose family still owns a substantial part of the island

We anchored in Port Ellen, a small town distinctly Victorian in character surrounding a curved beach. There is a tiny squat church of indeterminate age and another Victorian Evangelical Hall type of church. I wandered round the few streets of terraced cottages that surrounded the bay and admired the enormous tall wild growing Fuchsias presumably due to the warming Gulf Stream.

Fishing, tourism and much more excitingly Malt Whiskey distilling are now the main industries. A significant part of the population still speaks Gaelic.

# Hirta, St Kilda

The original islanders had had very little contact with the outside world, enduring a simple existence. They survived with a little farming of sheep, a few cattle and by exploiting the ample supply of seabirds. Indeed, many young men died falling from the cliffs whilst collecting birds and eggs. They had what is now referred to as an 'Utopian' existence of communal ownership, no need for money and a daily 'parliament' to decide what had to be done.

Following the introduction of tourism in the 19th century, young men began to emigrate and infant mortality rose to 80%, mainly because of what was called the 'eight-day sickness' which was later identified as infantile tetanus caused by the tradition of anointing the umbilical cord of the infants with Fulmar oil and sheep dung. The creeping decline in population became unsustainable. The islands last native inhabitants had to be evacuated in 1929.

Isolated in the North Atlantic, and part of the St Kilda Archipelago, this is a serene and spiritual place. The village is now owned by the Scottish National Trust and was being restored by them.

The original houses were of the 'Black House' type found on other Scottish islands, with no chimney or windows and sharing the space with the animals. The original ones were built in a group, but in the 19th century the village was rebuilt in the row of small single-story cottages which remain there to this day.

One notable feature, when approaching the island, was the huge number of 'Cleats' on the hillside. These are little stone built, long storage houses with grass roofs and were used to store puffins for the winter. They are exclusive to St Kilda. In the walls of these and along the stone walls surrounding the village are hundreds of the little St Kilda Wrens, bright and pugnacious. They are darker than our English variety and their loud calls are everywhere. There are also Soay Sheep, dark brown and more like goats, these little sheep had been imported from the island of Soay.

## Leith, Scotland

We had a Doctor changeover here. We usually had a new Doctor for each cruise, they had the cruise for themselves and their wives free, in return for Doctoring. We were unable to sail without a Doctor by law. The only qualification seemed to have been that they had Dr in front of their name! Although a consultant surgeon would be fine! The one we were dropping off was a retired Anaesthetist. He struggled the first time he was on. His son, a GP, had obviously told him that most non-specific illnesses were due to viruses. This time he had learned about Helicobacter Pyloris, the cause of most stomach ulcers, and any unexplained tummy problems were diagnosed as this. The trouble is that treating it uses a triple drug therapy and we soon ran out of the Proton Pump Inhibitors that protect the stomach from the treatment! At least he was pleasant.

The worst I encountered was a Paediatric Consultant. Tall, dark and extremely handsome, he would admire himself in the mirrors and have lots of photographs taken of himself in uniform. He was not married, but had been, and had children. He said he would like more. When he first came aboard, he required me to accompany him in the evenings. This was not due to my undoubted charms, I was well beyond childbearing, but because he was totally, socially incompetent and needed a prop.

He would rush into surgery, late every time, carrying a file and a mug of coffee, giving the impression he had just come from a very important meeting! His only relationship on board was with his computer, he spent most of the surgery peering at it and I came to realize that he was using it as a medical reference and also so that he didn't have to communicate with 'ordinary' beings. Unusually, we had a Travel Reporter on board and she wanted to interview the Medical Officer about Cruise Doctoring. (This was this Doctors first time on board.) So, my colleague Pearly and I listened in from the office next door.

'You are, what, in your thirties?' She asked

'No, in my forties.'

Pearly and I looked him up, he was in his fifties, and only a few years younger than me! We realized that the dead pan expression and black hair was due to Botox and dye!

## Mykines. Faroe Islands

This is a nesting site for seabirds and we were to circumnavigate it so that the bird enthusiasts could get a good view. The sea was pretty rough, so we couldn't get too close. It was still awe inspiring to see so many birds nesting on the basalt sea stack which is really just a large rock sticking out of the sea. There were Shearwaters, Fulmars, Gannets and many more. This particular cruise had been chartered by the Scottish National Trust and the passengers were of an entirely different breed. Very outdoorsy and stoical. Which was just as well because, just as we were leaving Mykines there was a loud screaming noise and the platform used for tendering operations came loose. It was normally made fast to the side of the ship and had been through many severe storms, but this time it was giving up the effort and had started to drop. This brought it within reach of the big waves we were suffering, tearing it away from the side of the ship, each wave pulling it further down and causing more damage. The Captain stopped the engines and a decision was made to cut it free, before it holed the ship or damaged the propellers. This was done by some of our stalwart crew, hanging in harnesses and using oxyacetylene torches, until the offending platform sank away into the deep. This cruise relied heavily on tendering, so we had to use the water sports platform to offload passengers, which was rather problematical. The deck boys practically lifting passengers on and off the tenders. It was either that or turn back. Divers were sent down when we docked in the Westman Islands to check there was no damage to the hull.

## Cruise around Hirta, Boreray, Soay and Dun

The St Kilda's archipelago is one of the most important nesting places for Gannets, Fulmars and Puffins. The island stacks were covered in what appear to be tidy rows of Gannet nests. They looked evenly distributed because each one is a bills 'stab' away from its neighbour which doesn't say much for their community spirit. The ship was mobbed and almost engulfed by these beautiful seabirds, as we circumnavigated the steep cliffs.

## Isle of Barra

Part of the Outer Hebrides, Barra has a pretty little cove with a medieval fairy-tale castle on a small rocky island in the bay; Kisimul Castle. The little village of Castlebay, named for it, has one or two shops and a tiny Fudge Factory, but little else. On a sunny day it must be delightful with beautiful views of the rocky harbour and little white sandy beaches.

It has the usual rumbustious history of ownership and clan wars. There are remains of an iron age settlement and like many of these islands it was claimed by the Vikings in the ninth century becoming part of the Viking 'Kingdom of the Isles'. Moving forward to the 15th century, following a particularly brutal period of clan wars and even piracy, James VI granted the 'Lairdship' to a MacNeill. They hung on to it until in 1838, when the island was sold to a Colonel Gordon, who expelled most of the inhabitants in order to replace them with sheep. It was finally sold back to a rich American MacNeil in 1937 and he, probably realizing that it had only a small track round the outside and an inaccessible rocky hinterland decided to bequeath it to the Scottish Government.

## Isle of Iona

Part of the Inner Hebrides and one of the original sites of early Christianity, its highest point is Dun, the site of an iron age hill fort. St Rhonan's bay is the main settlement. It's thought that the Monastery was founded here around 553 AD by a Monk Columba, it quickly became one of the most influential institutions to spread Christianity in the middle ages. There was an important Scriptorium, indeed, it is claimed that the 'Book of Kells' was started here. It also had the original high stone crosses with the circle in the middle, now known as the 'Celtic' cross, however, much of the original site was sacked by those unruly Vikings, becoming yet another part of their 'Kingdom'.

The present Abbey was built around 1203 and a Benedictine Convent was incorporated in around 1208.

In 1266 the 'treaty of Perth' returned the Hebrides to Scottish overlordships. Both the Monastery and Convent remained active until the Reformation.

In 1938, a George Macleod founded the 'Iona Community' an ecumenical Christian community for retreats and education; there are three centres, two on Iona and one on Mull.

This island is dominated by its Abbey, decidedly out of proportion with the rest of the buildings and habitations on these Hebridean Islands.

## Cruise to the Trenish Isles

Interesting cruising around these basalt flat-topped islands. Lots of seabirds and a lovely misty Scottish sunset. There is evidence of iron age settlements on some of these islands, and Lunga has the remains of a few Scottish 'Black Houses'.

The islands were bought by a Colonel Niall Rankin, an explorer and naturalist in 1938 and sold to the Hebridean Trust in 2000. They are now a sanctuary for wildlife particularly Puffins, which we could see skimming the water like little 'wind up' bath toys.

Having closed my journal on the last evening of my current contract, thinking there would be nothing else to write about, all hell let loose with a 'Code Alpha'. My cabin was just about at water level and I arrived on deck six, more out of breath than the poor individual who was in extremis with a severe asthma attack, the doctor stood there looking smug as I gasped for breath. It was all I could do not to wrest the oxygen mask from the patient. We took him to the hospital and tried stabilizing him for several hours, before deciding he needed to be in hospital on the mainland. We were on our way up the west coast of England and Wales at the time, so a helicopter was sent for. Helicopters were unable to land on our ships, so when it was nearly with us, we took our patient up to one of the lounges adjacent to the deck to wait. His wife was to accompany him and she was understandably terrified. I was incensed by onlookers and chased them away to find somewhere else to sit rather than gawk at a man who was likely to have a cardiac arrest at any moment. The helicopter was deafening as it hovered to one side of the swimming pool. A young doctor was winched down to assess the situation, then the patient's wife was winched up with him. Brave Lady. She lost a shoe and I noted for future reference that lace ups would be more appropriate. The Doctor then returned with the stretcher. We had the patient sitting up in order that he could breathe more easily, but he had to be lifted flat. He was taken first, then finally the Doctor was winched. Between every winching the helicopter flew off a little, before coming back for the next lift. All very exciting, for the observers. The patient was in hospital in ten minutes and we heard that he was comfortable within the hour.

# Chapter 6.

## *Norway and the North Cape*

### Alesund

This is an amazing slightly magical city built over seven islands which are now served by extraordinary tunnels. Capital of the Sunnmore district, in the northernmost part of western Norway and the most populated. A major port, it is full of boats of all shapes and sizes. Legend says a brigand Viking from a little place named Giske, north west of Alesund, founded the city, becoming the first Duke of Normandy. Apparently, he was too big for a horse to carry, with a personality to match. Fishing was the most important industry until oil was found in the North Sea and the boat builders turned to making vessels which were robust enough to service the Oil Rigs. There are lots of traditionally built brightly painted wooden Hanseatic Trading houses built around the port, close to the water, and some traditional houses climb up the steep hillside. The main part was rebuilt in the early 20th century, following a devastating conflagration in 1904 which destroyed the whole city overnight. Rebuilt with help from Kaiser Wilhelm, who apparently enjoyed holidaying here, it is now known for its consistent Art Nouveau Style. I visited the Jugendstilsenteret, originally a pharmacy, but now a visitor centre with a beautifully preserved interior, including a rather grand Pharmacists dining hall. Aalesund Church nearby, is large and solid looking.

It was pouring with rain, so although I had planned to brave the Gondola ride to the top of Aksla mountain which overlooks the city, I bought a punnet of strawberries to eat on the way back to the ship, instead, we were, currently, not allowed to take fruit on board because some of the crew have been leaving it to get rotten, making their quarters unhygienic!

## Ulvick

One full day at sea, and then Ulvick, Hardangerfjord. The views are stunning, steep, sheer rugged mountains rising from the dark blue waters. The northernmost part of the great Hardangerjokulen Glacier is here. Ulvick, meaning Farm, in old Norse, is a small village, with a pretty church.

In 1940, during the German invasion of Norway. the village was almost totally destroyed and three civilians killed.

The weather however was awful, cold and wet. The general feeling amongst the crew is that early May is a bit soon to be doing Norway. Still quite a lot of snow on the mountains, making the air icy cold.

## Bergen

Historically known as Bjorgun, which means 'meadow among the mountains. In the county of Hardaland on the west coast of

Norway, situated on its own Byfjorden and surrounded by seven mountains. Bergen is the second largest city in Norway and was the capital right through to the 13th century. Trading may have begun here as early as the 1020s, but it is said that the city was founded in 1070 AD by King Olav Kyrre. It became a major player in the Hanseatic League, a confederation of merchant guilds and market towns in central Europe. Started in a few north German towns in the late 1100s the league grew to dominate Baltic maritime trade for three centuries.

An interesting city, still the busiest port in Norway, it has the highest rainfall in Europe. Going ashore I passed the impressive 13th century Berghenhus Fortress. Further along I came to the wonderfully preserved Hanseatic League merchant houses known as the Brygen. Tall thin wooden buildings with planked walkways, very atmospheric and full of ghosts. These buildings burnt down and were rebuilt in 1702. Painted in the traditional colours of Norwegian wooden buildings, browns, oranges and grey's they look very pretty. I found a wonderful lace shop on the way into town, but was unable to find it among all the twists and turns on the way out! The rest of the town is modern, cosmopolitan, probably because they have suffered so many fires, which burned so many churches, often started by brigands or drunkards, but also during their very own civil war in 1198. It would be boring to list them all, but one in 1702 burnt down 90% of the city.

I met a group of infant school children dancing and chanting a nursery rhyme in the pouring rain wearing brightly coloured mackintoshes. Their teacher told me that they celebrate rain here. I don't suppose they have much choice!

They have the most extraordinary fish market, you buy

your fish alive and they chop it's head off for you. Quick and fresh! I saw my first deep sea angler fish there, extremely ugly, poor thing. Bergen is one of the most expensive places I know! I once bought a punnet of cherries for fifty Kroner, before I realized that that was around five pounds!

Bergen was occupied from the beginning of WWII. During the occupation a Dutch Ship named Voorbode, anchored in the harbour, and carrying 120 tons of explosives blew up, killing 150 people and damaging many of the historic buildings. Norway always had a very strong resistance movement.

## Olden

We set sail for Olden Nordijfjord, which is at the mouth of the Oldeelva River at the northern end of the Oldedalen Valley, the river is fed by a branch of the mighty Jostedalsbreen Glacier. Olden village has two churches, the 'Old Olden Church' a pretty wooden one built in 1759 and 'Olden Church' a red brick one built in 1934.

From here I went to see the Briksdalsbreen glacier, lying about 16 miles south of Olden along the Briksdalsbreen valley. This is one of the more accessible glaciers. It's amazing. We actually walked inside! Where the glacier is melting from underneath, it makes caverns that you can actually get into. The blue/turquoise colour in the cracks and fissures is magical. There were lots of Norwegian ponies, about 14 hands and stocky, taking tourists up the steep climb to the glacier in four-seater traps. Such patient, kind looking ponies, all a pale dun almost golden colour, with their manes hogged to show their dorsal stripes. This dark strip goes from the forelock of the pony, between its ears through the centre of the mane to the tail. One Mare had a Foal 'at foot' which was almost white, but already quite chunky, trotting along beside it's Dam. Unfortunately, there was a later accident involving these pony traps and I don't think they use them anymore. Like all native breeds, these ponies need a role in modern life to keep them going.

We drove back to the ship along the valley, past lakes which were a brighter turquoise green than I have ever seen before. This amazing colour is because of the particular combination of minerals brought down by the many waterfalls. They looked almost like beaten metal and slightly opaque,

The area was a popular place for artists at the turn of the century, indeed my family was introduced to Norway because my sons' Great-Grandfather was one of those artists. We have many Fjordic Landscapes in the family and have maintained friendships initiated from that time.

## Balestrand Sognefjorden

On the northern shore of the Fjord. Another pretty, tiny place not as large as my home village. Balestrand is an amalgamation of the Old Norse words for farm, 'bale' and beach 'strand'. Tourism and farming are the main industries and there are a few attractions laid on. There is the beautiful and famous Kvinkne's Hotel, bought by the Kvinkne family at the beginning of the century in order to cater for the many artists who came here to paint the wonderful scenery. Great-Grandfather was probably one of them. It has 200 rooms with balconies overlooking the Fjord, and many of its original fittings. There is St Olaf's, a copy of the traditional old stave churches, built in 1897 by an Englishwoman who came here to climb, but met and married a Kvinke. Sadly, she died before the church was complete. There's a much older church built on the little island of Kvamsoy in around 1280, a white stone Basilica with what look like very uncomfortable seats. Golden House Gallery keeps up the tradition of art and finally there is an Aquarium, small but interesting with a few Kayaks and canoes as well as a bakery on site.

Life must be very harsh, particularly in the long winters. I know the houses are warm and comfortable with all mod cons, but they are so isolated. The majority of the country consists of beautiful but uninhabitable mountains, with villages wedged into the flat areas on the shores of the fjords. Originally the only means of transport between the villages would have been by boat. It seems the churches and local community remain an important part of daily life rather like ours was fifty years ago. The young tend to emigrate to the larger towns for a few years, but I was told that many do return to raise their families.

Floating in the Fjord here, I spent a wonderful afternoon, on deck, keeping up the tradition of painting. Not quite up to Great-Grandfathers standard.

## Eidifjord, Hardangerfjord

We had to repatriate a member of the crew this morning, with a worrying stomach ache. We had been up nursing her since the early hours and had decided that she would be better in hospital in Norway, rather than risk taking her over to the UK, a thirty-six-hour sail. I went across on the tender with the patient, to meet the extremely efficient ambulance men who were transferring the poor girl to the nearest surgical unit in Voss. Having delivered her safely, I was too tired to go to bed, so decided to go ashore again and have a closer look.

Situated on the end of a narrow branch of the great Hardangerfjord, Eidfjord is another tiny farming village. Its large hotel seems out of proportion to the size of the place. There was a delightful girl in National Costume greeting passengers as they got off the tender and they were even offering helicopter flights. I had been given a seat on one of these, only to find that the clouds came down and it was cancelled. Instead I went to see the wonderful Vorringsfossen waterfall in the Mabodalen valley, it has a freefall of 182 metres or 597 feet into a narrow, wooded valley or gorge. The views are stunning.

They were building a quay, large enough for the Queen Mary to visit. Preparations were obviously in hand to welcome many more tourists here; this may have been the last chance to see the fjords in relative calm before the tourist hoards hit!

## Flam, Sognefjord

Another idyllic Norwegian settlement situated at the inner end of Aurlandsfjord, a branch of the vast Sognefjord, nicknamed 'The King of Fjords' it's the largest and deepest in Norway. The name Flam in Old Norse, means a plain or flat piece of land. It really is just that, a flat piece of land with a tiny harbour, surrounded by vast mountains on all sides. It's centred on the famous Flam Railway one of the steepest built on normal tracks, and running 20km or 12.6 miles. Started in 1924, it was finished in 1940. A branch of the Bergen line, it travels between Flam and the village of Myrdal, where it connects with a ferry. Wending through the stunning scenery of Flamsdalen, passing the dramatic Kjosfoss waterfall, it goes through 20 tunnels and has 8 stations with some spirals and a bridge on the steepest bits of the track. There were a couple of original trains on show for the enthusiast, and a modern new, forest green train on which some of our passengers had booked a trip. These trains give the place a flavour of the early pioneering days. In this country the shortest of journeys requires the most enormous engineering enterprises with tunnels and bridges on every road, particularly around the fjords. There is also a pretty wooden church built on the site of an earlier Stave church in 1670, it's a simple design, but nonetheless, a delightful little building.

## Gudvangen, Sognefjord

Another tiny place at the head of the very narrow and steep sided Sognefjord, which is at the end of an the even narrower Naeroyfjord where the river flows gently into the Fjord itself. The mountains are enormous here and rather overpowering with craggy granite outcrops and waterfalls, all reflected in the beaten metal waters of the Fjord. The triple Kjellfossen falls are just east of the village, it's one of the highest in Norway at 775 metre or 2,477 ft. The little village is on a low green valley floor. The sun catches the head of the fjord, but the sides are so steep that it can only reach the town for short periods, even in the summer.

There is now a 'Viking Experience' called Njardarheimr, where there are 'real' Vikings, exhibits and demonstrations.

## Stravanger

Stavanger, one of the oldest cities in Norway, is situated in the south west of Rogaland county. There may have been very early settlements here, from as far back as the retreat of the last Ice Age 10,000 years ago. There have been many archaeological finds from the early iron age, and also a stone age farm.

Still significant, for modern Norway, Stravanger is the site of a great naval 'Battle of Hafrsfjord' somewhere between 872–900 AD in which the victorious Chief, Harald Fairhair proclaimed himself King Harald I of Norway, thereby unifying the many little kingdoms into one country. There is a strange triple obelisk monument to this battle in the city. Despite all this ancient history the place is considered to have been officially founded in 1125, when the original Cathedral, now the oldest in Norway, was built by Bishop Reinald. Apparently, he may have come from Winchester in England. The original Cathedral ravaged by fire in the thirteenth century was rebuilt in a Gothic style, not very Norwegian. I am looking forward to seeing more of the decorative Stave churches.

Stravanger had grown to become an important Market Town by 1300, with fishing, shipping, shipbuilding and fish canning the main industries. Built over many lakes and inlets with bridges linking them. The core of the city called the 'Gamie' is mainly 18th and 19th century, painted traditional wooden houses and narrow winding cobbled lanes, reached by steep steps. Some of the old warehouses on the lower level by the harbour seemed to have walkways from their upper levels over to the old town. It's all very pretty, but the rest is rather a disappointment, a bit of a mishmash, with those traditional wooden cottages next to a concrete block of flats. The oldest museum in Norway, consisting of 8 buildings, is one example, with the latest development being a kind of rectangular 'brick' on pillars, very ugly. The more attractive Rog Art Museum does have some wonderful exhibits, including Munch, Christian Krogh, Elif Peterssen and Arge Storstein.

Offshore oil was discovered in 1969, and this has transformed Stravanger into the major metropolis it is now. Known as the oil capital of Norway, it has many international links, including banking, power companies and NATO's Joint Warfare Centre (JWC). It's considered one of the most expensive cities in Norway.

Medically this cruise had been pretty quiet, however towards the end, we had a little spate of poorly people. I sat up with one lady, trying to ensure she made the morning. We were not sure whether to order an ambulance or a Hearse when we Docked. Fortunately, we had the ambulance, and she recovered.

We had another lady who was terminally ill on this cruise. However, she was desperate to see the Norwegian Fjords before she died. How could we deny her!

## North Cape

A stop in Bergen before going up to the Lofoten Islands. The mountains were quite gentle for part of the way up to the Cape. We sailed inside the hundreds of outlying islands that make up this part of Norway, hoping this would give us calmer seas. We'd had rather a choppy crossing of the North Sea, which had kept us medics pretty busy. As we got further north, the mountains become craggier and more dramatic, with snow still clinging to the tops. There is open sea and sheltered bays, beaches and untouched islands. We saw a single 'Orca' with a large bent fin. If anybody shouts 'Whale', you have to be very careful not to be crushed in the rush of sticks, walkers and fast toddling old people. I always worried about the list of the ship. The Lofoten archipelago in the county of Nordland, is right up in the Arctic Circle. Lofotr was the name of the island, Vestvagoy, but later evolved into the name for the whole chain of islands. There are the most dramatic mountain peaks, straight out of Grimm's Fairy Tales, with trolls and giants hidden in the crags. There is evidence of human settlement as far back as 11,000 years ago, but actual archaeological finds only go back around BC 5,500. It is thought the first settlers were mainly farmers and fishermen. Indeed, the islands have been the centre of Cod fishing for 1,000 years. Cod come down from the Barent sea to spawn here. They are traditionally air-dried on poles and known as Stock fish.

In 1941 British Commandos landed on this island in order to get behind the German positions in a combined operation called 'Operation Claymore'.

## Harstad

Our first stop is Harstad, on the largest island Hinnoya, and Lofoten's most populated municipality in Troms county Halogaland, the northernmost, inhabited archipelago in the world. There are several bronze age cairns on the coast and archaeologists have found many bronze age artefacts on the peninsular. Harstad is mentioned in the 'Old Norse Kings, Sagas' as the power centre of the Viking age.

Trondenes district on the edge of the town has the northernmost medieval church in Norway, dating back to possibly the 13th century. There is an Historical centre next

door and nearby the 'Adolf gun', an enormous gun left from
the German occupation in WWII. The houses are traditional,
painted in the approved 'natural' colours of Norway, greens
and browns, with the occasional white one. Sitting on the edge
of the sea, a very pretty and romantic little town.

## Honningsvag

Honningsvag in Finnmark. This is the northernmost city of
Norway in Nordkapp municipality of Finnmark County.
Despite having only 5,000 residents it was declared a city in
1996. It's situated in a pretty bay on the south-eastern side of
the island of Mageraya. The famous, but underwhelming
North Cape Globe is on the northern side of the island. Settled,
like the other islands in pre-history, probably by fishermen, it's
a rich fishing ground.

There are three different peoples here. The Sami, who are
the indigenous minority, the Kven's, descendants of the Finns,
and the Norwegians. There were a few Sami people to
welcome us on the Dockside, in their bright red, blue and
yellow knitted and felted, embroidered clothes. True
Laplanders, they had some stalls selling rather badly made
sealskin slippers and horn bottle openers.

Not a lot else here! The houses are all rather plain and
built of timber. They are painted in earthy colours, but don't
look as substantial as one would have expected at this latitude;
although I'm sure they would have been very efficiently
insulated. The gardens were interesting, there is little attempt
at gardening. If it will grow, it is allowed to do so. There was
rough grass, wild flowers and a few hardy shrubs. In July there
were still a few tubs of daffodils and tulips and I saw one sad

looking Fuchsia. Florists do an excellent trade in all these northern towns. There are always lots of artificial flowers. What it must be like in the three months of winter when the sun doesn't rise at all, I can't imagine. I have noticed how many craft and hobby shops there are, both here in Norway and in the Baltic. They have to have something to do in the long winters!

Bamse, the famous St Bernard, WWII Mascot of the Norwegian Navy lived his early days here. He was owned by the Captain of the Whaling ship Thorod and went to sea from an early age. When the Nazi's invaded, the Thorod escaped to the UK and became a minesweeper. It was stationed in Montrose and Dundee, where Bamse became well known for his heroic efforts in keeping his crew together, picking them up from the pub when necessary, he apparently had a bus pass for this. He also took part in actual battles. He is the only dog to be awarded the Animal George Cross by the PDSA.

Virtually the only animals I saw here were dead animals. A stuffed polar bear, a stuffed reindeer, lots of skins, seal, reindeer and a few things made of fish skins. all rather smelly! There was even a harpoon on the quayside, making it very dangerous for any whale to venture within range!

We crossed the Arctic Circle, with its aforementioned underwhelming globe sculpture on a high cliff. We had a 'Crossing the Line' ceremony around the pool, all very silly and involving the Captain kissing a large fish! Everyone gets a certificate to say they have entered the Arctic Circle!

The most enthralling part of this trip was sailing close to the North Cape Horn; a rocky outcrop shaped rather like a rhinoceros horn. The engines were cut and we floated in utter silence at the top of the world. There were puffins skimming the water round us and reindeer on the hills. Magical.

The sun hasn't set for several days now. It's very strange how it sinks down to the horizon and then rises again at around 1.00 or 2.00 a.m. It's impossible going to bed when it's still sunny and warm. There's a real party atmosphere and we were still all drinking on deck at midnight!

## Tromso

Three hundred and fifty kilometres north of the Arctic circle, Tromso, again, is built over several islands, most of it on the island of Tromsoya which is connected to both the mainland and other islands by tunnels and bridges. It has a much milder climate than the rest of northern Norway because it lies in the gulf stream, they can even grow trees up here. Inhabited from the iron age by both Sami and Norse people. The Sami or Laplanders come from Norway, Sweden, Finland and the Murmansk Oblast in Russia. They are traditionally fur trappers, fishermen, and reindeer herders, about ten percent are still involved with the reindeer. Tromso soon became the centre for arctic hunting and there is a very nice sculpture of an arctic hunter by Sivert Donali on Stortorget in the market square.

The settlement was given the title, 'city' in 1794, by King Christian VII, despite the fact that at the time, it only had 80 inhabitants. The setting is stunning with snow covered mountains all around. There's a scary cable car up Mount Storsteinen which towers 420 meters or 1,380 feet above the city, giving wonderful panoramic views.

Tromso boasts the most northernly university in the world, established in 1968, they are careful to ensure a quota for the Sami.

During the 19th century Tromso became an important base for Arctic Explorers, like Roald Amundsen, to recruit their teams and plan their expeditions.

There's a Museum with an arctic alpine botanical garden, the most northerly botanical garden in the world. A short walk from the centre is the interesting Polaria aquarium experience, built in 1998 and there's the Northern Lights Observatory, founded in 1927.

I took an extremely expensive taxi ride over the enormous Tromso bridge which links Tromsoya to the mainland, in order to visit the famous 'Cathedral of the North'. This strange modern A frame structure, which looks so striking from a distance, is really no bigger than the average parish church. Built in 1965, the sides are built in a basic A frame and covered in what looks like a superior type of corrugated iron, presumably this is to prevent snow settling. The interior is simple, relying on the structure for impact with a stunning stained-glass window filling the whole of the A shaped east wall. There was a special service going on in aid of HIV and Aids, with the Crown Prince of Norway present and a Sami choir in their full national costume of bright reds, blues and yellows, with short frilly skirts, thick stockings for the women with pom poms on the shoes. The men wearing heavily embroidered jackets that had a sort of frill around the waist and a silver belt. Considering there was a member of the royal family present, the security was very relaxed. I was allowed to stand in the foyer, from where I had a good view of the service.

The earliest church was built here in 1252 named 'St Mary in Troms near the Heathens' (Sami) during the reign of King Hakon Hakonarson. There is also a more traditional Cathedral.

The city centre has the largest concentration of historical wooden houses in northern Norway, the earliest, 'Skansen' built on the remains of a 13th century rampart in 1789. They go right through to 1904, when wooden house building was banned in Norwegian towns because of the fire risk. They sit quite happily next to the modern developments.

I went for a walk and there were very few cars, the roads I walked soon turned into grassy tracks. There is little gardening up here in the Arctic Circle, lack of light, and short summers; however, it was a beautiful sunny day, everybody was out on their verandas or having barbeques and there were some attractive gardens, including a few that consisted of carefully cultivated lawns of dandelions!

Unfortunately, we had an outbreak of D & V on this cruise, with its usual strict hygiene precautions by the crew, and the sick passengers not happy with the extended isolation needed to get the outbreak under control. I did my best to explain that even though they now felt well, they would be shedding virus for 72 hours.

## Ny Alesund. Spitsbergen or Svalbard

The town is situated on the Brogger peninsular on the shores of the Bay of Kongsfjorden. Coal was discovered here as far back as 1610, by a passing whaling ship, but the first shaft was not sunk until 1909, followed by a hut in 1912. The Kings Bay Kull Company was founded in 1916 by Peter Brandal, and 30 workers were sent to the bay to start construction of the little town. The mining company had a chequered life and was nationalized in 1933. There followed a series of fatal accidents culminating in a disastrous explosion in 1962 which killed 21 miners, putting an end to mining in Ny Alesund and precipitating a political crisis in Norway called 'The Kings Bay Affair'.

Kongsfjord Telemetry Station opened in 1967, it's involved in space tracking, since then it has been joined by 15 more permanent research stations run by agencies from 10 different countries, all concerned with environmental and earth sciences.

Between 1925–28 four attempts were made to reach the north pole by air from Ny Alesund. One involving airships, and led by our friend Roal Amundsen, managed to fly over the North Pole, landing in Alaska, another did reach the Pole but crashed on its return.

There are a few raised cinder roads, an old train, no longer running, a post office and shop. Largely populated by scientific, outdoorsy types, the houses looked as substantial as a painted wooden house can, a few dogs tied up outside and lots of skidoos or snowmobiles. I went for a little walk, unwittingly taking my life in my hands as I didn't register the polar bear warning signs until I was half a mile out! Everybody is supposed to carry a gun for protection against polar bears and doors must not be locked in order to ensure places of retreat if a bear should mistake anyone for a meal.

The arctic tundra is mossy in character with large areas of low growing alpine plants, mainly in pink. There were eider ducks and lots of noisy arctic terns, one of which dive-bombed me because it had built its dug out nest at the side of the path. I could hear one songbird which sounded like a lark, but I was told was a snow bunting which is a summer visitor. Summer! if this was England, it would be a freezing winter's day! The skies were clear and blue, but the wind was bitter.

There are three protected areas on the island, Blomstrandhamma Bird Sanctuary, Fongjorden Bird Sanctuary and Ossians Nature Reserve. There are Svalbard reindeer and if you're lucky you may see an arctic fox.

The scenery is stunning, we were docked in the little bay and with the engines stilled all was silent and rather eerie. Two enormous turquoise glaciers appearing to tumble into the glassy still water.

## Longyearbyen. Spitsbergen or Svalbard

The largest settlement and administrative centre for Spitsbergen is located in Longbear Valley on the shore of Adventifjorden on the west coast. It's actually the world's most northerly settlement of more than 1,000 people, originally named Longbear City after an American Boston-based businessman who bought the mining rights and set up the Arctic Coal Company in 1916. Mining operations have moved to nearby Sveaguva at the head of Mijenfjord and workers commute from Longyearbyen. Because of the permafrost, they have to mine uphill, into the mountains and use a sort of Ariel tramway to deliver the coal to the Dock in Hotellnstot. Following a difficult financial period during WWI, the Arctic Coal Company was bought out by Norway's Store Norske Spitsburgen Kulkcompani or SNSK. Still producing substantial amounts of coal today, the SNSK removed elements of what had been a Company Town and introduced a modern democratized system. There have been a few disasters here. In 1918, 11 people were killed by Spanish Flu and in 1920 they had a serious explosion in one of the mines which killed 26.

Although they were not affected by the German Occupation of Norway, the British evacuated 765 people to Scotland, leaving a few to carry on with the production of coal. However, in 1943, the place was almost destroyed by German 'Kriegsmarine' ships. All was rebuilt and they continue to export coal to mainland Norway and Canada.

Again, this is a young community with an average age of 35. Men outnumber women and there are plenty of children! Facilities for these families include schooling for all ages, with two kindergartens, which have high polar bear fences surrounding them, an hospital, swimming pool, gym, cinema and club as well as a community church, which is more coffee shop than church. Many supposed 'essentials' were tax-free in the shops and I took advantage of this by buying a very expensive pair of serious walking shoes. I am still using them daily.

I went on a coach around the island, visiting a 'Dog Yard'. Tourism has become an important part of the economy, and dog-sledding a substantial part of that. The yard had a hundred friendly huskies, who loved being petted by the visitors. Each had a kennel on legs with its name painted on and the dogs were chained to a little post in front. We were assured they do run free some of the time. The Huskies were looking a little moth eaten because they were moulting their extremely thick winter coats in great chunks. There were a couple of handlers who looked after the dogs, one of them, a girl, wearing a sealskin coat. We were shown the thick seal blubber, very high in calories, that has traditionally been fed to Huskies, although they did say that this was supplemented with a modern dry kibble for the skinnier dogs. A white husky named Tampax!

had given birth to only one pup seven weeks ago. She was thirteen! We all had a cuddle! There was also a litter of four two-day olds we could only 'peep' at

Polar bears can be a real problem here, and the butchered seals were strung up onto an enormously tall wooden tripod to dry and to prevent the bears taking them. All the timber used has to be imported, because nothing grows higher than an inch here.

Before we left, we were given a snack of dried seal, served with sour cream. Unexpectedly delicious!

Nowadays there are several Scientific establishments and amongst them, the Svalbard Global Seed Vault, an international storage centre for rare seeds.

Whilst up in the polar region we were privileged to see a few polar bears. We had a wonderful Captain, Olav, who got very excited when he spotted wildlife and announced it on the address system. We spent some time with the engines cut floating silently in atmospheric Magdalena Fjord, where there are two enormous glaciers, we were lucky enough to spot polar bears hunting on the edge of these. They are difficult to see, pale against a pale background and we had crowds of spotters all along the ship. Once spotted we could see them quite clearly with binoculars. Fortunately, I was on the bridge with the Captain and he kindly lent me his. Another time there was one hunting on an ice flow who disappeared through the ice before finally coming up with a seal. Later, on the same day a bear was seen calmly swimming past the ship.

On the way to Magdalena Fjord we passed a large sandbar absolutely covered in Walrus, there wasn't an inch to spare. One popped up beside the ship to have a look at us, his tusks were enormous.

Later, we had a gentleman presenting with indigestion, which on ECG turned out to be an acute MI or heart attack. However, we were one and a half hours by helicopter from the nearest hospital in Spitsbergen. He was deteriorating fast, so we gave him appropriate drugs, called them in and hoped for the best. We don't have landing pads on our ships, but I felt that we managed this lift a little better than the last, in which the poor patient had been ogled at by passengers. We cleared the lounge before taking him up, keeping him in the warm until the last minute when he was hoisted into the helicopter on a stretcher. Unfortunately, this gentleman was the sole carer for his severely disabled wife, so that left us to care for her. She was unable to move anything except her left hand, which meant hoisting her to get her up and to put her back to bed. This raised many issues of the feasibility and expectations of our passengers. Emails flew back and forth from the main office for days. We had many passengers who expect the deck hands to carry them up and down gangways in their wheelchairs, horrifying me, having worked in the NHS where no lifting is allowed, and putting our crew at great risk. How willing should we be to meet the sometimes, unreasonable demands, of those who have the misfortune to be disabled? This lady was lovely, but if the sea had been rough, there is no way we could have managed the hoist safely, and, of course, we would have been in real trouble if we had had another inpatient needing our intensive care. I am told that regulations have now changed and crew do not lift any more.

# Chapter 7

*Up the Baltic.*

## Elsinore, Denmark

First mentioned in 1231 AD, by King Valdemar the Victorious and called Helsingor by the Danes, this is just a small trading port in eastern Denmark. Only five kilometres across from Sweden on the straits of Oresund it became strategically important during the middle ages when King Eric of Pomerania built the original Krogen Castle. in 1492, there was another Castle across the strait in Helsinbort, Kerrman Castle. This enabled the city of Elsinore to extract tolls from passing ships who also used the town for provisioning. Thus, Elsinore became very rich and this can be seen in the many grand buildings around the Harbour including the updated and newly named Krönborg Castle, rebuilt by King Fredrick II to become the grand Renaissance building it is now. It is supposed to be where Shakespeare's Hamlet is set.

In 1658 Denmark lost the southern Swedish provinces, however, the tolls lasted until 1857 when they finally lost control of the straits. The subsequent loss of income led to a period of great poverty, until Shipbuilding and ferries across to Sweden became increasingly profitable. There is now a large and impressive bridge.

In the older part of the city the buildings are mainly wooden and the streets narrow, they are painted in soft greys and greens. There is an enormous square with an old Carmelite Priory together with its Baroque Church. A pretty town with some very modern architecture juxtaposing with waterfronts that remind us of its early trading and fishing heritage.

## Copenhagen

Capital City of Denmark on the eastern coast of the island of Zealand. Originally a Viking fishing village, it has had a troublesome history. In the middle ages the Hanseatic league constantly attacked it and even our own dear Admiral Nelson knocked it to smithereens in the early nineteenth century. After suffering plagues, fires and constant attacks, it has grown into a very elegant, largely neo-classical and sophisticated city, I saw the 'Little Mermaid', which is 'little', through the crowds, and then went on to the Amalienborg Palace, the home of the Danish Royal Family. The Palace is built with four classical façades surrounding an octagonal courtyard. Every day at twelve o'clock the Royal Guard, known as the Denkongeligue Livgarde, 'Change the Guard,' marching through the streets to the Palace, in their red, blue and black uniforms with crossbands and Busbies! Then I went on to the Christiansbörg Palace, which is still the seat of the Danish government. Visitors have to wear soft slippers over their shoes. Wonderful extravagant interiors, some very contemporary, reflecting the different eras of rebuilding following several fires. The last rebuild in 1928 is in a lavish Baroque style. There were some beautifully decorated rooms, with little painted birds on the walls and chairs. The chandeliers were stunning, mostly contemporary, and there were some tapestries from the nineties, which I found rather harsh. This palace is used for visiting dignitaries, royal audiences and formal entertainments. There are some wonderful earlier buildings, the Börsen or Stock Exchange, built in brick and with an amazing spire made from the tails of four dragons.

On another visit I walked to the Tivoli Gardens with a friend, only to find them closed. Long walk, we had tried to get hold of some of the slot rental bicycles, but couldn't find any that weren't damaged. However, it did give us the chance to get a real flavour of Copenhagen. Very smart and rather expensive with lots of pedestrian shopping streets and 18th and 19th century architecture. We came across an amazing Spider Sculpture in one of the squares near the Tivoli. Over nine metres high 'Maman' by Louse Josephine Bourgeois, represents the nurturing, spinning and weaving instincts of her own mother! There are several of these sculptures around the world and I was to come across it again in my travels. It never failed to intrigue.

I did get to the Tivoli Gardens on a subsequent trip. The second oldest amusement park in the world, built in 1843, it would be better seen in the dark, which is rather late on a summers evening in Denmark, however it was fun seeing all the rides I wouldn't go on if you paid me.

Instead I went for a trip on the Canal, lots of low bridges making taller people duck. There's an area full of houseboats, the Slusenhaven Harbour with lots of roof gardens and geraniums in pots.

The city has an allotment area, on the outskirts, just like the original Victorian ones. A summer escape, each one has its own summerhouse, some of which are extraordinary flights of fancy. They are all tucked in behind wrought iron gates.

After setting sail, we had a very sick patient who needed overnight intensive nursing. However, we organized for an ambulance to be waiting and repatriated him in Helsinki in the morning. Once he was stabilized, he would be flown home. One of my jobs was to contact the insurance company for the passenger. I've had many an argument with Insurance companies, when people hadn't fully disclosed health issues. Nightmare.

## Gothenburg, Sweden.

The second largest city in Sweden and the country's main harbour. Situated on the south western coast and founded as a fortified, largely Dutch trading colony in 1621, by King Gustavus Adolphus. The city council actually consisted of four Swedes, three Dutch, three German and two Scots, largely because they needed a range of engineering skills in order to drain and build on the marshland. There is still a strong Scottish influence in the city, including a 'Chalmers University of Technology'. Fishing was the main industry until 1731, when the Swedish East India Company started trading here and the city prospered.

I went on a trip round the islands of Sweden's wild and rocky coastline. The countryside is heavily wooded except where large areas of pinkish granite are exposed. We went through Kungalv; a very picturesque town of 17th and 18th century houses, all built of wood in traditional style and painted in pretty pastel colours. We visited a couple of fishing villages, one called Skarhamn with its interesting Nordic Watercolour museum and another, Kladesholmen. The islands are linked by bridges and are heavily populated during the short summer months they have here. The harbours are packed full of fishing and recreational boats. There seemed to be hundreds of tiny rocky islands in the bays, which they call 'inland seas'.

## Helsinki.

Capital City and the largest in Finland, situated on the Gulf of Finland and built over an amazing three hundred and fifteen islands. I found it absolutely charming. On my first visit I had expected yet another elegant sophisticated city, and it is; but it also retains some of its ethnicity and a simplicity of its own. Established as a trading town by King Gustav 1st of Sweden in 1550 in order to compete with the Hanseatic trading countries, a plan which failed and the town remained in the backwaters. They suffered again in 1710, when plague killed most of the inhabitants. It was only when Russia defeated Sweden in the Finnish Wars of 1809 annexing Finland as the Autonomous Grand Duchy of Finland, did it begin to prosper

There is a market by the harbour. The stalls have lots of hand-crafted things like knitting and felting; some of the felting reaching extreme heights of fantasy, evidence of how the Finns spend their long dark winters! I also visited the undercover market. A traditional food hall, with lots of unfamiliar fish and smoked things!

Having lunch by the harbour one day, I watched a performance of Cats and a Poodle doing their 'tricks'. Why didn't the cats run off? They just went back to their baskets after each performance!

On another visit there was an outrageous 'punky' type band using a motorbike for a drum and another group of smaller children singing, who appeared to have no attending adult.

There is a wonderful Neo-classical Lutheran Cathedral, like a wedding cake, white with tiers culminating in an immense dome. Not what one associates with the Lutherans. Built in the 19th century, it seems to be a compilation of Russian Orthodox and Lutheran. Inside it is very ornate and beautiful, with masses of Icons. One Icon which was under glass, had personal items of jewellery pinned all around it, wedding rings, lockets and even a pair of sapphire earrings!

Another time in June, Senate square, in front of the cathedral, had some sort of spring festival. Everybody comes out to play in the short summers. There was an enormous stage and lots of stalls, national costume and music. I bought a bunch of Lilies of the Valley which would have been finished a month ago at home. The Lilac is only just out too.

## Oslo.

What a noble, expensive Capital City which according to Norse saga's was founded in 1048 and established as a place of trade by Harald Hardrada, although there is evidence of an earlier Christian presence. It became the Capital of Norway under King Haarkan V, around 1300. It was he who started the building of the Akershus Fortress. I walked to the city through this old Fortress which overlooks the Harbour, still inhabited by the Norwegian army, it's very angular, fierce looking, but somehow still managing to be picturesque. Originally the city was on the other side of the bay, but after a series of fires, in 1624 the king, Christian IV of Denmark, demanded the city be rebuilt near the fortress and it was renamed Christiana in his honour. An important centre of trade and a member of the Hanseatic league, the city continued to prosper, maintaining enduring personal unions with both Denmark and Sweden throughout. Finally, in 1814 it gained autonomy and became the capital of the Independent Kingdom of Norway. It was renamed Oslo in 1925. It remains the economic and governmental centre of Norway.

Built on a square grid with long straight roads, there is an abundance of modern sculpture around. Most of it seems to be dedicated to motherhood in the form of naked, buxom women and their pretty naked children. There was a lovely traditional circus around the harbour with decorative wooden travelling vans.

The main thoroughfare is extraordinarily wide with the Royal Palace one of the first buildings to be built on independence, by Hans Linstow in 1824 sitting importantly on a grassy hillock at the end, with wide steps leading up to it. Then there was the majestic National Theatre with its many fine sculptures including one of Ibsen at the entrance.

## Stockholm, Sweden.

Stockholm, Capital of Sweden, has been occupied since the stone age, but was founded as a city in 1252 by Birgar Jarl. It's an amazing place, built over fourteen islands at the intersection of the Baltic sea and Lake Malaren. In fact, there are over a thousand islands in the whole archipelago. I went into the medieval old town, known as Gamla Stan, which is where the

Royal Palace was built in a Baroque style after the destruction by fire in 1697 of the original Tre Kronor Castle. These medieval streets are very narrow with the large cobbles typical of the Baltic together with pink and grey granite paving slabs. I climbed up to the Palace, buff coloured and curved around a forecourt, where there was a 'Changing of the Guard'. There were soldiers in steely blue helmets that splintered the sun and dazzled the onlookers. Some had bayonets fixed and held at right angles to the body in a very threatening manner that was belied by their badly fitting uniforms and fresh complexioned, boyish faces. In the palace forecourt there was a mounted band playing melodies for the crowds. Beautifully matched and turned-out horses, with gleaming coats, heavyweight Bays in the front with the Timpani, then a row of Greys and finally a row of bright Chestnuts with white socks, carrying the Brass.

Stockholm is famous as the home of the Nobel Prize where the King of Sweden presents the Laureates in the Concert Hall followed by a celebration Dinner in the City Hall. For some reason the Peace prize is presented in Oslo.

The sail out was beautiful, through those lovely islands and their accompanying islets, many with traditional wooden houses and boats drawn up to the front. A boat here is probably a necessity, like having a car parked outside. It felt rather like sailing through a picture book story from Swallows and Amazons.

## Back on board and sailing for St. Petersburg

Sailing up the Neva, we passed through ugly industrial areas and the sinister grey hulks of submarines. The Russians have had a few disasters with submarines, losing a whole crew when they were unable to bring one up from the depths in the Arctic circle. More recently they had another case in which the international community managed to cut one of their subs free using a British Robotic rescue vehicle. Despite this they appear very attached to these disquieting machines.

It's May and I find it fascinating to look out of a porthole and see the sun just setting at midnight.

We dock on the Lieutenant Schmidt embankment on the opposite shore to the Russian Cruiser Aurora. Symbol of the October Revolution, she is now preserved as a museum. We are right by the beautiful wrought iron Blagoveschensky Bridge. Always welcomed by a brass band, we would stay for a weekend. This gave us time to visit the ballet, opera or the many wonderful palaces open to tourists.

Wow! this is a fairy tale city. The overall symmetry and design of the place is mind blowing. Built largely on marshland in around thirty years by Peter the Great in 1703 using conscripted serfs and the most fashionable European architects of the time, the Tsar was determined to have a city to equal any in Europe. My first visit was on the 300th Anniversary of the founding of the city, and we got thoroughly caught up with the celebrations.

The city seems to consist mainly of palaces along rivers and canals. It is stunning, but in 2003 it didn't pay to look too closely. Most of the major buildings, particularly those along the River Neva had been restored, painted in pastel colours, and those not yet restored have an attractive shabbiness about them. The churches and important palaces have outlandish roofs, onion domes and pinnacles in real gold leaf and coloured tiles. I remember a large Church with a collapsing Dome next to our berth. By my last visit in 2006, it was also being restored. I particularly noticed it because the Large

Dome was silver and I watched with fascination as it was re-silvered.

The scale of the city is enormous. The main roads are around eight lanes wide, built for horses and carriages probably. They make the M25 look small, and crossing is a dangerous business! There are still lots of horses, with young girls riding around, informally dressed, chatting to the boys. Local livery or riding schools? I don't know. There were several original battered carriages in the Winter Palace square with tired or bored looking horses waiting for customers.

On one occasion I discovered a part of town not usually seen by tourists. A couple of blocks back from the Schmidt Embankment is a busy shopping area, with bustling streets and modern shops, although still with no shop fronts as we would know them. Window dressing is not a career to take up in Russia! One enters what looks like a multistorey car-park and on climbing some stairs you come upon a full shopping precinct, very disconcerting. Particularly difficult if you can't read the signage outside, which presumably advertises the shops within. I also discovered a covered food market, which was wonderfully stocked with everything from Caviar, through meat and vegetables to Honey. The vegetable stalls were works of art with produce piled high in pyramids of carefully graded colours and sizes. There was a wonderful exotic spice stall.

It seemed as if St Petersburg, particularly, is moving into the 21st century with an almost alarming speed. I asked a guide whether it was 'better' now than 'before'. She said it was no better for the elderly who sometimes have to survive on $30 a month. Apparently, there was much poverty in the countryside and the average salary is $250. Practically what I would spend on one grocery shop at home. The main problem was the widening gap between the rich and poor. I had heard once before from a taxi driver that nobody pays their taxes, and that only about 25% is ever collected. You can't run a country on that!

The Hermitage and adjoin Winter Palace are amazing, every room stunning and more beautiful than the last with gold leaf and marble, massive lapis or onyx vases. An afternoon barely covers a small section of this enormous hoard. I have never seen anything to match it.

The Russians, then, didn't appear to have got a grip on tourism. The Hermitage was so crowded, I was anxious for the safety of some of the fabric and artefacts. In Copenhagen, we had had to put on soft slippers, so as not to damage the floor, here, we all just scuffed through, pushing and shoving to see the exquisite detail, though there were some pretty fierce older Babushkas, who hissed at you if you tried to take photos or leant on anything. Wandering through those magnificent rooms, heavy with gold leaf and crimson, I always found the floors amazing. They are in parquet, using many woods, sometimes in twenty or thirty colours. It is also sobering going around the extensive galleries to suddenly come across a particular picture, made famous on biscuit tins, such as the 'Lady in Blue' by Gainsborough. I found myself casually passing world famous Breughel's or early Italian works of art. I remember thinking, 'so that's where it is'! There is also a collection of early impressionists.

Something I was curious about was why they don't clean their silver. There was a massive Funeral Casket with various grand accoutrements in solid silver but looking like blackened steel.

The windows all had slightly grubby incongruous rouched nets, presumably to protect the contents from the sun.

Coming out, we got caught up in a parade. The buses had been moved and it took some time to round up the party. What a privilege to be there at that time.

I had many weekends in St Petersburg and saw a little more every time, and, in later trips, I did explore further and although the side roads remain elegantly wide and the houses of architectural merit, they looked battered and dowdy, with boarded up windows. The downpipes for rainwater are enormous, about ten inches across and made of lead, very battered and obviously original, they delivered the rain straight onto your feet. Looking through torn net curtains however I spied signs of real poverty and shabbiness behind these grand houses.

The pavements are so broken and rough that you have to watch your step. They say Russia is a big brother state, but if you break your neck on the pavements, it's nobody's fault but your own! The road near our dock had tramlines which had risen proud of the road. The old trams still ran over it, and I have an enduring memory of the Police Skoda's with sirens sounding like braying donkeys!

I went to the open market by the "Church of the Spilled Blood". This extravagant church is Neo Classical, but manages to hark back to a medieval style of Russian Architecture. It was built by the Imperial family as a shrine to Alexander II, who was assassinated on the side of the Gribeodov canal here in 1881. The canal itself was narrowed so as to include the actual site of the Assassination. The Domes are a fantasy of gold and coloured tiling. It should be garish, but somehow it isn't. Inside the shrine, on the actual spot of the assassination, the walls are encrusted with Topaz, Lazurite and other semi-precious stones. The rest of the interior is covered in the most wonderful art nouveau style mosaics depicting stories from the New Testament.

The improvements I saw over the three years that I visited were substantial. The roads were being tarmacked; the previously elevated tramlines now sit neatly in the road. No more invigorating Taxi journeys in ancient Taxis, skidding round the potholes with no seatbelts.

On one trip to St Petersburg, I and my nursing colleague went to the ballet, Giselle, absolutely wonderful. The Russian Ballet is so very expressive. However back on-board we had an emergency. An elderly gentleman was in heart failure. The Doctor had been managing it since the patient came in at around seven in the evening. We worked on him in our little hospital until three a.m. when the doctor decided that we would have to send him into hospital. An ambulance was called, unrecognizable as such to western eyes. I went with the patient, but was anxious for his safety as the ambulance appeared to have little equipment on board, no defibrillator, oxygen, nothing! This was 2003 and we travelled through the scruffy suburbs with lights and horn sounding, to an area which looked as if it was undergoing demolition, rubble all around. We came to an industrial styled steel gate among the rubble. The driver sounded his horn but nobody came, it was ages before somebody shuffled out to unlock the gate to let us through.

The hospital was unbelievably shabby. I particularly remember standing outside an intensive care room, which had square white tiles on the wall with grubby grouting and nothing else as far as I could see. The gentleman's wife had arrived by now and however hard I tried to persuade the Nurse in charge, she wasn't allowed to be with her husband. I left her there, sitting on a little metal chair outside the shaggy torn soft-board doors.

When we have this sort of situation, a ship's agent would be there in every port to help smooth things out. It was he who organized the Taxi for the gentleman's wife and who got me back to the ship.

I was just having a reviving cup of tea and trying to describe what I had seen, when we were called to one of our young hostesses, Mia. I delightful girl, she was convulsing. When we stayed overnight, some of the young crew go to a nearby nightclub and she had been out all evening. We worked on her for three hours, using up all our anti convulsive drugs. She was very ill and we were desperate. She had to be transferred to hospital. My colleague and the doctor went with her to what turned out to be a Lunatic Asylum. This was how the Russians classified what they had decided was a drug issue. My colleagues reported that the patients, some of whom were ventilated, had rubber urinary catheters draining into a communal bowl and that they were all strapped down to the beds. Fortunately, the Doctor had the authority to refuse our patients admission to this ward and she was taken to an intensive care unit. As she was strapped down apparently screaming, my colleague had to be restrained physically from releasing her. She arrived back terribly upset. Neither of us had had any sleep at all.

Fortunately, by mid-morning our young patient was stabilizing and had been released from her bonds, but it was decided that she would remain in hospital and that the ship would have to sail without her. As her employers, the company had responsibility for her welfare, so I was volunteered by the Captain to stay with her and attempt to deal with the Russians.

I did a quick pack and still in my uniform complete with silver buckle, was taken to the hospital Mia was in. The uniform was clearly perceived as a threat by the unit manageress whose own garment consisted of a white see through wrap that barely covered her bottom! It also gave them the impression that I was going to nurse Mia. This would have been unsafe, as absolutely nothing was recognizable, the drips, glass bottles with rubber tubing, no pumps. I was unable to understand drug regimens or anything. Fortunately, by now we had a young Medical Student who spoke good enough English and he was able to calm the situation and explain to the huffy Russian nurse that I was only there to do the 'soft' nursing and as a companion. He was obviously in love with Mia at first sight!

The ward was a real eye opener. It had four scruffy beds with stained mattresses, the sheets were of a thick green material, as were the towels. There was one other patient who was unconscious but not ventilated. There were no screens, so the only privacy I could provide for Mia was to hold up a sheet for her. When I asked for a bowl to wash her, they didn't know what we were talking about. Apparently, they don't wash their patients; eventually our Student friend found us a rag, which I was able to wet at the only sink in the room. We did our best with this.

Equipment was virtually non-existent. There was a monitor for heart, oxygen saturation and suchlike, some glass bottles for fluids, some extremely old and dirty ventilators and what looked like an oxygen concentrator on the wall which was clearly new. The atmosphere relaxed and I was offered the empty bed next to Mia, I had been up for thirty-six hours by now and I did try to get some sleep. I visited the only lavatory I could find, some distance down a wide empty corridor. The Lavatory was unbelievably dirty, the bowl black, with bits of cut up newspaper for toilet tissue lying over the floor amongst the overflow from a lidless bin for sanitary towels. On my way back I passed a cadaver partially covered on a trolley.

One of the things I was able to do for Mia was to put her on the bedpan. The only bedpan. The only facility in the 'sluice' was a running hose of cold water into a flat, wide stainless-steel sink. I never did find out what one was supposed to do with the 'solids'. Loo paper and anything else 'intimate' had to be put into a small open topped bin in the middle of the ward. There were, of course, no rubber gloves. The only measuring device was a marked bottle, there were no detergents and the water, which was brown, slopped onto my feet. There were a few shelves in the sluice, which was about six foot by ten foot, and on these were two plastic urine bottles, next to a row of glass bottles which appeared to be the ones used for intravenous fluids!

Lack of equipment due to financial restriction is understandable and will draw forth sympathy, but the attitude to patients were uncomfortably alien. The patients were there to be cured and this was done skilfully with the equipment available. Nobody would have understood the concept of 'holistic' care.

The ward itself was dirty from the floors to the bed, to the sticky fly papers over the beds. Open bins were commonplace and so were the flies. I wondered about cross infection rates, and was only too pleased that Mia did not need to be ventilated.

After a slightly difficult discussion the next morning with the Doctor looking after Mia, we managed to discharge ourselves. He suggested that the only findings in her blood were cannabis and alcohol. Prior to her admission we had felt that she had probably been slipped something much stronger as her reaction was so serious and I was arguing this; when I remembered where I was, and shut up!

We were transferred to a private hospital. These were beginning to spring up to cater for the increasing number of tourists and they valiantly tried to match what they perceived to be the European expectation of medical care. The food was brought in from a local restaurant. Very nice. However, they only had four beds, so extras like me had to sleep on examination couches in the offices.

The poor gentleman I had delivered earlier had sadly died. Fortunately, his wife had been strong enough to insist on being allowed in to see her husband following his death, not something the Russians do apparently. She was brought back to the same clinic as Mia and I. The Nurses there, with the best of intentions were trying to give her a sedative injection. Since this eighty-year-old woman was also sleeping on an examination couch, I didn't think this appropriate, she was in shock. We managed to get her to eat some soup and I arranged for some recognizable sleeping tablets she could take later if she wanted.

So now I had two people to care for. The clinic wanted to keep Mia in for a few days, but I insisted that I was taking her out on the Tuesday. There was some urgency to getting Mia out of Russia as soon as possible. The drug issue could well have developed into a major incident.

The medics caring for her were very keen that she should have further tests, and we were taken to yet another hospital where an ECG and MRI were done. This hospital had top class equipment and I had the feeling that they were trying to prove a point. Indeed, it was obviously undergoing full renovation. We walked underneath angle grinders showering sparks onto us from above, as they remoulded what was obviously yet another palace. No health and safety here. I was informed that this was to be the new military hospital!

For our last night in Russia Mia and I were moved to an apartment in readiness for a four-a.m. flight the next morning. We stopped outside the usual shabby, old, elegant building near one of the canals. This one had massive security doors which opened onto a wide crumbling staircase. Five flights up and we entered another world; a state-of-the-art apartment with jacuzzi bath and all mod cons. There were some rather incongruous very retro cheap plaster ornaments which made us smile.

For some reason I had not been allowed to leave the clinic. If you carry a seaman's book, you don't normally need the usual visa's and that includes for Russia. However, they would not let me out and I had determined to buy a Russian wedding present for a friend at home. So, as Mia was comfortable and safe to leave, I ordered a Taxi by phone and was taken to my chosen shop, opened up just for me, where I bought a large bottle of Vodka in a wooden painted Doll. Appropriate for my friend!

We were picked up next morning for our flight to Frankfurt where we had a long wait, so we had a doze in a local park. Then a flight to Munich before another to Rostock in a little thirty-six-seater. There we were met by the agent and taken to re-join the ship docked in nearby Anemone.

Mia's friends had clubbed together for me to have a beauty treatment as a 'thank you', for looking after her. Very kind.

I had been anxious about leaving our newly widowed passenger in the Clinic, but her son flew out to rescue her the next day. We kept in touch for many years.

## Tallinn, Estonia

One of the oldest capital cities in northern Europe. It has an horrendous history of being occupied. Initially claimed by the Danes after a successful raid by Valdemar II in 1219, followed by alternating Scandinavian and German rule. As the northernmost member of the Hanseatic League, during which it was known as Reval, it was quite prosperous. In 1710 it capitulated to Imperial Russia, whilst retaining some autonomy. In 1918 an Independence manifesto was proclaimed, quickly followed by German occupation. There was a War of Independence with Russia and in 1920 the Tartu Peace Treaty was signed, making Estonia a Republic. That didn't last long, because during WWII, in 1940, they acceded to Soviet Russia until they were occupied by Nazi Germany. On the German retreat they were annexed once again to the USSR becoming the Capital of Estonian SSR. Finally, in 1991, they became a fully independent Republic.

The Old town is charming, One of the best-preserved Medieval Cities in Europe. It has winding streets climbing the hill to the old Viru gates, with their cone shaped roofs. The centre remains an intimate, pretty place, almost like something Brueghel might have painted, spoiled by the large ugly tower blocks, containing the much-feared Russians, visible on the outskirts. I went to the wonderfully ornate Alexander Nevsky

Cathedral with its five onion domes and gilded Pediments, named after a Saint Alexander, who won an important battle on Lake Piepus in 1224. Building started in 1894, the architect was Mikhail Preobazhensky and it was finished in 1900. It was so hated by the Estonians as a sign of Russian oppression that it was nearly pulled down in 1924; but it was too solid and they didn't have enough money so it was allowed to deteriorate. Notwithstanding its beginnings, it was carefully restored when Estonia finally gained its independence. The inside is fantastically ornate with an enormous altarpiece of the Apostles and beautifully decorated mosaic arches.

There was lots of lovely Amber for sale in the many little shops and a heavy sort of linen, which was quite fashionable when I was there.

On another occasion I went for a meal with friends to a medieval restaurant in a medieval square with medieval wenches in national costume. There was Bear on the menu! but I had a delightful pudding made with Mascarpone Cheese with a little bit of condensed milk and Rose Petal essence, very medieval!

The city changes every time we visit. There was a Music Festival on one occasion when several cruise liners were in, they are definitely opening up for the tourists. Although it was Sunday, the town was very crowded, with lots of people in traditional costume, some selling roasted nuts in the streets. All very upbeat. They had just joined the common market

## Riga, Latvia

The Capital of Latvia, the history of Riga is really complicated. Situated in the Gulf of Riga on the River Daugava, and ideal for trade, everybody wanted a slice.

Originally settled by the Finnic Tribe it was the centre for Viking trade during the middle ages. It took a lot of crusades and much persuasion for them to abandon paganism and Pope Innocent II sent a Bishop Albert in 1201. He started the fortifications and then Roman Emperor Philip invested Albert with the Principality, under the Holy Roman Empire. The populace had to pay taxes to the Bishop until a settlement was reached in 1225. They finally accepted the reformation in 1552 and there is a nice story about a group of iconoclasts who declared the statue of the Virgin Mary in the cathedral to be a witch. It was put to trial in the River and declared a witch because it floated. It was then burnt at the stake.

In 1621 Latvia came under the King of Sweden, Gustavus Adolphus, and stayed that way until Russia besieged what was a plague weakened City in 1710. Throughout all the centuries of war and changes of power, the Germans maintained a dominant position. However, in 1905 there was a revolution, largely unsuccessful, led by the leader of the 'Latvian Democratic Workers Party'. It was the beginning of Latvians call for Independence, which they finally attained in 1918.

Occupied like so many of these Baltic States by the Russians and the Germans in both world wars. The Soviets maintained an iron grip on Latvia, with the KGB Headquarters or Stura Maja based in Riga. It is now a museum dedicated to the many occupations of this land. The 'Singing Revolution' started in 1987, finally led to full independence for both Estonia and Latvia in 1991.

There are some lovely old buildings in Riga. The Castle founded in 1330 has been constantly rebuilt and augmented throughout the ages. Today it is the official residence of the President. St Peters Church with it's amazing tiered wooden spire and the beautifully ornate stepped gables of the headquarters of the delightfully named 'Brotherhood of Blackheads', not for spotty teenagers but for an association of unmarried merchants and shipowners, active from the mid fourteenth century right up until 1940. I believe it still exists elsewhere. There is a distinctly 'Dutch' style to the buildings, tall and narrow, prettily painted, and with stepped, sometimes really ornate, gables. The older streets are cobbled with stone buildings and arches.

However, whilst leaving through the large sea walls, we felt a sizable thump. Later that day, no-one was allowed down to where the beauty parlour and Gym is. I managed to 'peak,' there were lots of tarpaulins covering an area, thankfully, above the water line, and the sea was relatively calm. There was some discussion as to whose fault it was, the Pilot or the Captain. I believe, the poor captain lost his job.

## Warnemunde, Germany

Founded in 1200 and situated in the Baltic sea on the mouth of the River Warnow. An attractive German seaside town with beautiful beaches; originally a fishing village, it still has some pretty fisherman's cottages, one of which was occupied by Edvard Munch, the Norwegian painter who painted 'The Scream' who stayed here for a short while. There's a rather solid brick church in the square. and a Modern Curved roofed building known as the 'Teapot', an example of East German Modernist Architecture and currently filled with Restaurants. During the summer it was very crowded and busy, with kites and flags everywhere in the pearly blue sky surrounding the lighthouse at the end of the bluff. The river runs through the town, a wooden bridge built over it with market stalls and coffee shops on its banks. A friend and I went for a meal in the evening. Any kind of Fish!

## Kiel Canal, Holtenau/Brunsbuttel

Built in 1895 it took nine thousand workers eight years to construct the canal, starting at Holtenau on the Baltic. It was formally opened by Kaiser Wilhelm 1. It was rebuilt and widened in 1914 in order to allow Warship's to transit. It is still one of the busiest in the world saving two hundred and fifty nautical miles round the Jutland peninsular.

The bridges along the canal are no less than forty-two metres high and our ship was one of the few Cruise Ships able to navigate it. Uniquely captivating and incongruous, sailing regally through beautiful spring fields with a few feet of water each side of the ship. It was a lovely blue day and the German 'Father and Son' festival was on, so the canal was crowded on both sides with families enjoying the weather. Everybody waving at us, lots of rather jolly shouting and hooting as we sailed majestically past. The Captain couldn't resist the odd hoot back! Especially when a man waved a Norwegian flag at us. Ear splitting! We had to go under several of those bridges, when it really didn't look possible and we held our breath until we were through. There were ferry ports all along, the little ferries themselves dashing across in front of us, a little like playing 'Chicken', all great fun. It took eight hours of sailing through sixty-one miles of fields, with a lock at the beginning and one at the end, at Brunsbuttel, which let us out into the North Sea!

# Chapter 8

## *Iceland, Greenland and Canada*

### Vestmanneayjar, Westman Islands

These islands are part of an archipelago on the south west coast of Iceland and, apparently, they were named after slaves captured in Ireland by the original Viking Settlers. These slaves were known as 'The Men from the West'. There are fifteen islands and many rock stacks and skerries, like a load of pimples on the sea, but Heimaey is the only one to have a permanent population. A small island with a neat little harbour between two volcanic outcrops, the main industry is fishing and the production of fish oils; the smell of this pervades the whole island. There was an eruption here of the volcano Eldfell in 1973 and the whole population was evacuated to mainland Iceland.

Steep cliffs and lots of Fulmars nesting. Seabirds everywhere. Sertsey, the newest of these islands only 'popped up' from the sea in 1963, and is of enormous geological and botanical interest, in both the formation and colonization of a new island. We circumnavigated it, which enabled us to see the layers of ash and the larvae flows. There were already small areas of vegetation, the seeds brought in on the feet and faeces of seabirds.

## Reykjavik, Iceland

The settlement of Iceland began in 874 AD when the Norwegian Chieftain Ingolfr Armason became the first permanent settler, other Scandinavians joined him bringing their slaves or serfs with them, most of whom were of Gaelic origin. The country was run as an independent commonwealth, one of the first. However, after a period of strife they acceded to Norwegian rule in the 13th century. In 1397 the 'Kalmar' union united them with Denmark Norway and Sweden. They finally gained full Independence in 1918 and founded a republic in 1944.

Reykjavik, the first settlement in Iceland and the Capital city, was founded as the official trading centre in the late 18th century. The middle of the city has a very 'pioneering' look to its buildings, not unlike that found in New Zealand. Brightly painted clapboard and corrugated iron Victorian buildings together with a pretty little square. The rest of the city appeared to be built in a modern modular, Scandinavian style and sprawled for miles.

The landscape is quite extraordinary. Covered in a thick volcanic crust that has been cracked and lifted by ice, making it into a vast, black, craggy plain leading to the island's many volcanoes. The mosses and lichens, which have colonized these larva fields, are like thick custard spread over the surface and running into the cracks. They come in an amazing variety of colours and are interspersed with wild flowers, mainly saxifrages and a few grasses.

I went on a trip to the Blue Lagoon, an area of thermal, salt water activity. As we approached through the Lunar landscape, the steam rising from these lagoons was visible from a great distance. This area has been developed as a resort with treatments for a variety of skin conditions, with Spa's, Sauna's and a shop. There were whole families crowding into the communal changing rooms and they paid scant attention to modesty, a little disconcerting for us Brits. The pools were quite busy. The outside temperature was around ten degrees, so one made a dash to get in. It was one of the most delightful experiences of my life. The water was a milky blue with a gravel bottom. There were white silica deposits on the black volcanic rocks surrounding an interlocking string of pools. There is one area where a geyser spouts water up into the air and this was the hottest part. It was like a giant luxury bath shared with friends. We were actually served blue cocktails by a young man in a one-piece bathing suit and sporting a dickey bow tie.

## Greenland
## Narsaq, Greenland

Nasdaq translated from Kalalau, Greenland's language means 'Plain' referring to the shore of Tunulliarfik Fjord and the flat area where the town is situated. It has been occupied for Millenia and there are remains of a 1,000-year-old Homestead on the outskirts of the town. Today there is a Town Hall, Church, Primary School, several other educational facilities including the only Food Technology college in Greenland, an Internet Cafe and an Hospital. Narsaq has always been a major trading centre for Greenland because of its deep harbour. Until 1900, seal hunting was the main economy but it has since transferred to fishing. This is the one area where they have sheep farms and the first Brewery was established in 2004. I was surprised by the rocky and barren character of Greenland. I wasn't sure what I had expected, large pine forests, perhaps. In fact, there are no trees at all in this area. But splendid mountains covered in northern tundra. Around eighty percent of Greenland, the largest island in the world, is covered by permanent ice. Only the edges are habitable. However, it was summer when we visited and the flowers were lovely, mainly because they all have to flower together in the short summer. The houses are wooden, all building materials have to be imported, and are painted in bright colours.

## Narsarsuaq

Southern Greenland, on first appearance seems like a barren place. The main airport for the island is here, consisting of an airstrip, one hotel and a coffee shop. It is because of this airstrip built by the Americans at the beginning of the second world war in 1941 and known as 'Blue West' that the settlement exists at all. I walked, with a friend into 'town' which was about a mile, the weather was unexpectedly warm and we were plagued by small flies which kept getting up our noses and into our mouths. By the time we reached the coffee shop together with its inevitable museum, built in the original air force barracks, we were pretty uncomfortable.

There was some evidence of subsistence fishing, but not much else. The scenery is stunning, with mountains and a splendid glacier that some of our braver passengers went off to climb. The wild flowers of Greenland are beautiful in summer with enormous Harebells, a short version of the Willow Herb, which is the national flower and numerous saxifrages and cotton grasses. There are also lots of brightly coloured Lichens and Mosses. The temperatures in summer can reach twenty-four degrees centigrade, and can go as low as minus thirty-nine degrees centigrade in winter. However, this is one of the more temperate areas in Greenland and they do have trees. In fact, they have a whole Arboretum known as the 'Greenlandic Arboretum' where there is an enormous collection of trees from the Arctic and Alpine areas of the whole northern hemisphere.

## Qaqyartoq.

Inhabited continuously since prehistoric times, a rich variety of cultures have settled here. The Saqqaq people established themselves 4000 years ago, followed by the Dorset and, of course the Norse in the late 10th century; later the Thule who were an Inuit people joined the Norse in the 12th century. In 1775 the Danes took over, naming the town Jullianehab after their queen of the time.

The main town of South Greenland, it is the size of a small village with brightly painted wooden houses built up a rocky slope. There is a small village square with a whale fountain, the water spouting from its blowhole. A pretty little wooden church beside a babbling river and wild flower meadows. There were some interesting Inuit carvings on rocks by the road. This was an art project led by Qaqortoq artist, Aka Hoegh and started in 1993 in which eighteen other artists from Finland, Sweden, and Norway were asked to contribute. Originally there were twenty-four but now there are around forty of these primitive style carvings.

The main industry has traditionally been Seal hunting and tanning, now they rely heavily on tourists. It was bitterly cold, but some of the Inuit children were running around half dressed and eating ice creams. There were one or two shops selling rather expensive but poor-quality souvenirs and a museum, built in an old Blacksmith shop which focused on Inuit carvings of whales' teeth, I found some of this Inuit art somewhat grotesque, mythological creatures with several heads muddled up with arms and legs. Nearby there is an ancient harbour building, built in 1797 in Denmark, it was shipped flatpack style back to Qaqyartoq and reassembled. Nothing is new!

We had a Choir on board that evening. They sounded like the local WI, singing hymns in the very complicated Inuit language. They were dressed in Sealskin tops and trousers with bright embroidery and smelled pretty strong!

## Nanortalik, Greenland

Nanortalik means 'The Place of the Polar Bears' and is situated on an island in Southern Greenland on the shores of the Labrador Sea. A pretty little village of brightly coloured houses perched around a rocky bay. It was the first part of Greenland to be settled by the Norse and the last to be settled by the Inuit. Founded in 1770, in 1830 it had to move three kilometres north to secure better harbour facilities. There is little left of the original settlement.

The harbour was full of icebergs and the sea crystal clear, with towering mountains all around. There are several tiny settlements surrounding Naortalik itself, sometimes with no more than twenty inhabitants. Crab fishing, seal hunting and surprisingly a goldmine, are the small industries here. And they have a forest! Known as the 'Qinngun Valley Forest' it has Birch and Pine reaching several metres.

I had to take a patient to the hospital. She had had a CVA or stroke and was very poorly. Because the Island is Danish, there are large subsidies and I was surprised to find a charming little Cottage Hospital, with a pretty veranda overlooking the sea and a bright clean interior. They only had one other patient, so our passenger received lots of attention, probably relieving the boredom, and I had no anxieties about leaving her there. Repatriation was going to be their problem.

Most of the people in Iceland are Eskimo's or Inuit as they are now called. The rest are Danish. I found some interesting facts about the Inuit. They are actually physiologically different. They have no septum in their noses and proudly demonstrated this by squashing their noses flat. They told us that this with their high cheekbones helped prevent frostbite. Not sure how. The men don't have any beard growth only a little moustache and they don't go bald! Because they eat few vegetables and no dairy, their digestive system can't cope with such things. Their main diet consists of Seal, Whale and Musk Ox. There are no overweight Inuit, they are all permanently on the Atkins diet!

Their National Costume is Sealskin Trousers and Jerkins, with embroidered white under-boots that reach to above the knee and then covered by more sealskin decorative boots. The women add colourful beaded tabards over the jerkin.

## Canada

Five days at sea dodging Hurricane Maria, before landfall in: Newfoundland. St Johns.

St Johns is the Capital and leading city on the eastern tip

of the large Avalon Peninsular on the island of Newfoundland, part of Canada's Province of Newfoundland and Labrador. Originally inhabited by people of the 'Maritime Archaic Tradition' they were gradually displaced by the 'Dorset Culture', known as L'nu or M'kmag, who in turn were replaced by Inuit and the 'Beothuks', Paleo Eskimo tribes. In medieval times Norsemen settled on the peninsula, leaving some interesting archaeology.

A chap called John Cabot sailed into the harbour in 1497 AD. One of the oldest European settlements in North America, it tended to be seasonal with Fishermen setting up camp during the summers. Early in the 16th century Cabot came back with his son, Sebastian, sailing into the harbour on the Feast Day of St John the Baptist. So that's how it got its name.

In 1583 an English 'sea dog' named Sir Humphrey Gilbert claimed the area as England's first overseas colony under a 'Royal Charter of Queen Elizabeth 1st'. Unfortunately, he was lost on the way back to England, and no plans were made to settle the territory. However, by 1620 Fishermen from England's West Country were controlling most of the east coast here and sometime after 1630, St Johns was established as a permanent community. The population was slow to grow and in 1665 the Dutch attacked, but only stayed for a short time. This upset the colonists, so they built some defences, and in 1673 when the Dutch came back, they were valiantly repelled. Twenty-three men led by an English Captain Christopher Martin, against three Dutch Warships.

However, 23 years later, the French sacked the place in the 'Avelar Peninsular Campaign' of 1696 and when the English reinforcements finally arrived, they found only a pile of rubble. The French were pretty determined, attacking again in 'The Siege of St Johns', capturing it in 'The Battle of St Johns' in 1708. The harbour continued to be fortified during the 18th century. Finally, during 'The Seven Years War' in North America, there was a concluding fight against the occupying French in 1752, the 'Battle of Signal Hill' in which the British, under the command of Colonel William Amherst retook Newfoundland. The Cabot Tower, from this era is still on the top of Signal Hill.

The 18th century saw a slow and steady growth with Seal hunting and Salmon fishing. The town remained a Garrison and served as a Naval Base during the 'American Revolutionary War'.

The dreadful weather did it's best to dampen the delightful atmosphere of this charming place. The old clapboard houses are painted in bright colours and are mostly 19th century terraces, with bay windows and attractively hipped roofs. In the past the city had suffered from several devastating fires, culminating in 'The Great Fire' of 1892.

They are very proud of their contribution to the dog world and have statues of the Newfoundland and Labrador dogs in the city where the only other thing of note is the handsome Roman Catholic Basilica of St John the Baptist, with its twin towers.

In 1901 Guglielmo Marconi received the first transatlantic wireless signal here, transmitted from his station in Cornwall England. It was also the site for the embarking or culmination of early Transatlantic flights.

In WWII both the Royal Navy and the Canadian Navy were stationed here, together with an Army Air-force base. This was transferred to Canadian control in 1960.

Newfoundland and Labrador were badly affected by the

collapse of the northern Cod Fishery, but were miraculously rescued by the large number of oil fields discovered nearby. Indeed, this led to an explosion of the population in the 1990s.

## Corner Brook.

On the west coast of the island of Newfoundland, the 'city' is located in the 'Bay of Islands' at the mouth of the Humber River. It's the most northern city in Atlantic Canada.

Originally inhabited by those Maritime Archaic tribes mentioned before and followed by the Inuit. There was a brief European contact around 1000 AD when the Vikings had a little look round. Then in 1776 Captain Cook surveyed the area. However, it remained a small village of Fishermen and Lumberjacks; in the 19th century it still only had a population of around 100 inhabitants.

This is still a bit of a dump. An industrial town, sprawling up the hillsides, with smoky chimneys and a population of less than 20,000. I popped into 'town'. The taxi dropped me off at what he called the 'Shopping Mall', which consisted of two shops. One selling quite nice 'crafty' things and the other an 'Antique' shop without one genuine antique. The only highlight was a wonderful Newfoundland Dog sitting in the doorway of the shop. I must say he wouldn't move and didn't look particularly intelligent!

## St Pierre & Miquelon

An archipelago of eight islands, but only these two are inhabited. Miquelon is really two islands itself, separated by a long narrow sand isthmus or 'Tombola'. Its particular anomaly is that it remains a self-governing territorial overseas

'Collectivity of France', situated in the north Atlantic near Newfoundland and Labrador, actually in the entrance to their Fortune Bay.

Portuguese Jaoa Alvares Fagundes landed on the islands in 1520, but they were made a French possession in 1536 by Jacques Cartier on behalf of the King of France. The indigenous M'kmag peoples were known to visit it, as did Basque and Breton Fishermen. In 1670, a French Officer annexed the place after he found a French Fisherman's camp. For some reason the British Navy harassed them, pillaging the camps and destroying the ships. By early 1700 the island was again uninhabited. They tried to sort themselves out with 'The Treaty of Paris', which put an end to the seven years' war and St Pierre and Miquelon were returned to France. However, the Americans were having their Revolutionary war against the British and Britain again invaded and destroyed the little colony in 1778. They sent the entire population of 2,000 back to France. Squabbles continued, the islands going back and forth between Britain and France until after the 'Hundred Days War'. This was when Napoleon having escaped from Elba, had another go at being the boss of everywhere. The islands, by then uninhabited, with nothing left standing, were finally returned to France. It was resettled in 1816 by Basques, Breton's and Normans. In 1910, the fishing industry collapsed and many of the settlers emigrated to Nova Scotia and Quebec.

They had to find something else to do and found another 'industry' in smuggling. During the American 'Prohibition' years a massive amount of whiskey and other beverages found their way to America via these islands. The end of prohibition led to full economic depression.

During WWII, they allied themselves to Vichy France, but Charles de Gaulle seized the Archipelago for 'Free France'.

We arrived here in the most dreadful rain. The town itself was a rather uninspiring little fishing port. The one notable thing was the bright, often garish colours of the clapboard houses. Red, yellow, purple and green!

They have the only Guillotine used in North America in their museum. It had to be shipped from Martinique for the purpose of executing a murderer in 1889. Why didn't they just hang him!

## Saguenay River and Fjord

This is a National Park, located where the Saguenay River meets the St Lawrence River in Quebec. Whales are known to congregate in the estuary with the St Lawrence River, and we were up at 06.00 hours in the hope of seeing some, but as usual, I seemed to miss them every time, though there weren't many.

Aborigines are known to have inhabited the area for thousands of years, the first European to sight it was that chap Jacques Cartier in 1535. However, it wasn't settled permanently until 1840, when the fur traders moved in. Later Lumbar became the main industry until, by the end of the 19th century the forests were seriously depleted. In 1970 the Quebec Government began acquiring the land and the 'Saguenay National Park' was opened in 1984.

We had a wonderful sail up to the Fjord in lovely weather with pine covered slopes on both sides. The Fjord isn't quite as steep as the Norwegian ones but we sailed to the end where there was an impressive white statue at the top of the enormous cliff, 'The Notre-Dame-du-Saguenay Statue'. I was lucky enough to be on the Bridge at the time. The engines were cut, enhancing the silence of the wilderness and our very good Ship's 'Tenor' sang Ave Maria, a cliché, but Magical!

# Quebec

Quebec City is Capital of Quebec Province, one of the thirteen provinces and territories of Canada. Set on the north bank of the St Lawrence River where it joins St Charles river, surrounded by fertile plains and valleys with the 'Lawenton Mountains to the north. One of the oldest European settlements in North America. The old town, known as 'Vieux-Quebec', is the only North American fortified city.

Explorer Jaques Cartier started those fortifications in 1535, staying during the long winter, before sailing back to France, returning in 1541 with the intention of establishing a settlement. Unfortunately, he encountered such hostility from the indigenous Iroqoian people, he was forced to abandon it after one year. However, those original inhabitants died out, partly due to wars with the Mohawk Tribes and maybe also due to imported European diseases.

Finally, it was successfully settled in 1608 by an explorer and diplomat called Samuel de Champlain, who built a new settlement on the site of the abandoned Iroquoian village. He stayed for many years administering the little town, named 'Stadacona' at the time. It became the cradle of Francophone North America. Primarily a fur trading outpost, there was little growth for decades, probably because men outnumbered women significantly. Indeed, later in 1663, 500 French women were imported to help redress the balance. In the meantime, English Privateers led by a chap named David Kirke managed to capture the place at the end of the Anglo-French War in 1629. Now, Champlain argued the legality of this as 'technically' the War had ended. So, in 1632 King Charles of

England agreed to return the lands to France, providing Louis XIII paid for King Charles' wife Dowry. This was the 'Treaty of Saint-Germain-en Laye'.

Quebec was the headquarters from which many raids emanated in an effort to expel British traders in what became the four French-Indian Wars. The last named 'The Seven Years War', when the city was captured by the English in 1759. Led by General James Wolfe, in 'The Battle of the Plains of Abraham', carried out on those imaginatively named plains which lie west of the defensive walls of the city. Then in 1763 the French 'ceded' all its North American possessions in 'The Treaty of Paris', 'swapping' them for Guadalupe, and its rich sugar cane industry. At the end of French rule, the city had around 8,000 inhabitants.

Distinguished by its monumental buildings, fortifications and affluent homes of stone. There are shacks in the suburbs and its surrounded by forest's villages, pastures and fields.

The American Revolutionary troops attempted to 'liberate' the city in the 'Battle of Quebec'. In 1775 their failure ultimately led to North America having two distinct political entities. Fearing more attacks in 1812, when the United States again attempted to annexe Canadian lands, the inhabitants of Quebec constructed the Citadel and fortified their already strong defences. They needn't have bothered because the Americans never attacked again. However, the citadel maintained a large British Garrison.

In WWII Quebec hosted two major conferences in 1943 and 1944, attended by Churchill, Roosevelt and other very important people. Much of the D-day landings were planned here.

Most of Old Quebec is built on the edge of a plateau and

there are an awful lot of steps. The city is on two levels with those long flights of steps and a Funicular to the upper level where there is an enormous Gothic Victorian Railway Hotel, 'Chateau Frontenac', red brick with slate turreted roofs which dominates the skyline. Wide boulevards and long tall 19th century terraces. This part of the city is still surrounded by the fortified walls, now topped with a wooden walkway, allowing wonderful views. There are steep hills in all directions.

French and Catholic, there is the Cathedral Basilica of 'Notre Dame, Quebec', in contrast to the sweet little Church, 'Notre Dame-des-Victories' built in 1687. The Parliament building is monumental with a large clock tower. And on top of 'Cap Diamant' and adjoining those 'Plains of Abraham', the Citadel itself is still occupied today and houses the residences of the Governor General and Head of State.

The lower town has narrower streets and 18th century foundations, the buildings tall and stone built, difficult to date, with some attractive roofs, cobbled streets and pretty squares. There was an elegant French feel with lots of tubs of exotic flowers including Canna Lilies. There were a couple of very impressive wall paintings, skilfully drawn and amusing, covering the whole sides of buildings.

Canada remains a Federal Parliamentary Democracy and Constitution, with Queen Elizabeth as Head of State.

## Nova Scotia

The name means 'New Scotland. It's one of Canada's three Maritime Provinces and the smallest. Originally inhabited by the Mi'kmaq people, the first Europeans arrived in 1605. French colonists established the areas of Newfoundland &

Maritime Provinces bordering the Atlantic and including Quebec. These together became known as Acadia.

The British conquered in 1710 and the 'Treaty of Utrecht' formalized their claim. They weren't very friendly, because they expelled those original French Colonists in 1755, replacing them with New England 'Planters'. More 'Loyalist's' (Americans Loyal to the British) arrived in 1867 and Nova Scotia became one of the founding Provinces of the Canadian Federation.

Continual squabbles during the 17th and 18th centuries significantly influenced the history of Nova Scotia. French, English, Scottish, Dutch and Mi'kmaq argued over the lands in six separate wars. After the third 'Father Rale's War of 1725 the Mi'kmaq signed a series of peace and friendship treaties with the British, allowing them rights to hunt and fish on their own lands.

The fighting continued and Edward Cornwallis brought in some more British to re-enforce their claim. During the American Revolution of 1775–1783, Nova Scotia was known as the 'thirteenth' American Colony but they were rather ambivalent about joining America. It didn't help that American 'Privateers' devastated the Maritime economy by stealing the ships and looting almost every town outside Halifax. Unfortunately, the British were forced to surrender to Canada and their French Allies in 1781. However, it was still considered to be a safe place for around 33,000 'Tories' or 'Loyalists'. As part of this 'Loyalist' migration 3,000 Caribbean Blacks arrived, founding the largest 'Free' black settlement. However harsh treatment led to around a third of them returning to Africa, where they settled in Sierra Leone, naming their settlement 'Freetown' in 1792.

In 1848 Nova Scotia became the first British North American Colony to achieve a 'Responsible Government', allowing them to make some of their own decisions.

After the 'American Civil War', Premier Charles Tupper, led Nova Scotia successfully into the Canadian Confederation in 1867.

Nova Scotia became a world leader in building wooden ships and indeed, owning them. Samuel Cunard who founded the famous Cunard shipping line was born here.

## Halifax

Capital city and county in the Canadian Province of Nova Scotia, deriving its name from George Montague-Dunk, 2nd Earl of Halifax in 1759.

This seemed to be a city that has lost its way as far as architecture is concerned. There is a nice boardwalk along the harbour, with a few flat-topped shopping areas. There are a few 'preserved' older buildings, including the inevitable result of all that squabbling, another 'Citadel', but the town appears to be a mish mash of architectural styles, with terraces of older clapboard houses next to ugly car parks and high-rise buildings. I was informed that they were bringing in new planning requirements in order to address the situation; limiting the height of buildings in the older quarter.

I went sailing in the harbour on a 'Tall Ship', not that we did much actual sailing. We viewed the harbour and all its industry from the sea. There is a pretty residential area with old houses on the opposite bank in the town called Portsmouth. We were told a couple of interesting stories. One was about the disaster in 1917, when a Norwegian ship collided with a

French Cargo ship, in the 'narrows'. The resulting explosion killed 2,000 and destroyed the Richmond area of the city. Another, happier story was about an Indian Princess on the Portsmouth side, who fell in love with a sailor. The Chief put a curse on the crossing, to keep them apart saying the bridge would collapse three times, once in a storm, next time silently, and then finally just collapse: the first and second came true. They got the local Chief to lift the curse when it was rebuilt for the second time!

The Nova Scotian's are very proud of their Scottish ancestry. Bagpipes welcome the ships and Kilts are worn!

Back to Dover, England and I had my Brother and Sister-in-Law on board for lunch. It's nice to touch base occasionally. There are often parties of travel agents being entertained on turnarounds, so, some of the Restaurants remain up and running.

Although I actually only live about twenty miles inland from Dover, we are usually too busy for me to take the time to go home. Apart from checking the delivery of drugs ordered, we usually had a new Doctor to introduce ourselves too, and, if he or she (we only had two 'she's' in my time) hadn't been on board before, we had to explain the systems and show him or her around the clinic and hospital.

My next trips were to take me to France, the Mediterranean, and the Black Sea.

Printed in Great Britain
by Amazon